HOW TO START YOUR OWN
THEATER COMPANY

D0063940

HOW TO START YOUR OWN
THEATER COMPANY

Reginald Nelson

CHICAGO
REVIEW
PRESS

Library of Congress Cataloging-in-Publication Data

Nelson, Reginald.
How to start your own theater company / Reginald Nelson.
    p. cm.
Includes index.
ISBN 978-1-55652-813-2
1. Theater management—United States.   2. Theater—
Production and direction—United States.   3. Congo Square
Theatre Company (Chicago, IL)   I. Title.

PN2291.N45 2010
792.02'3—dc22   2009042271

Cover design: TG Design
Cover artwork: Antoine Savolainen, © Images.com/Corbis
Interior design: Pamela Juárez

© 2010 by Reginald Nelson
All rights reserved
Published by Chicago Review Press, Incorporated
814 North Franklin Street
Chicago, Illinois 60610
ISBN 978-1-55652-813-2
Printed in the United States of America

For Mama

"I can take any empty space and call it a bare stage. A man walks across this empty space whilst someone else is watching him, and this is all that is needed for an act of theatre to be engaged."

—Peter Brook

CONTENTS

FOREWORD

In 1988, upon graduating from Northwestern University, seven other former students and I started the Lookingglass Theatre Company in Chicago. We had acted with and directed one another while at school and had come to share a common process and an aesthetic that we loved. We wished to continue to develop this vision, longed to be able to support ourselves through our work, hoped to be celebrated, dreamed of having our own theater, and were determined to be the Next Big Thing. We pooled our life savings, begged and borrowed, and began what was to be the greatest challenge of our artistic and professional lives: launching (and, more important, sustaining) a not-for-profit ensemble theater company in arguably the most competitive city in the country.

In 2009 Lookingglass celebrated its 20th season, and it's still going strong. We've created more than 50 original plays, all world premieres; toured productions across the country; expanded our ensemble to more than 20 actors, writers, directors, and designers; and maintained a stable of diverse artistic associates. We've built a permanent home, a completely flexible, state-of-the-art black box theater in a historic building on Michigan Avenue; grown our annual operating budget to more than $3 million; cultivated a dedicated staff, a generous and passionate board of directors, and an army of interns; and launched an outreach and education program that currently reaches and teaches 15,000 students a year.

I am proud of what we, as a company, have accomplished—but I must confess that it was against unbelievable odds. The stories of financial crisis, loss of faith, bitter disagreements, devastating reviews, horrific audience attendance, emergency room visits, and brink-of-disaster saves are too numerous to detail. I can't tell you how many wonderful companies with untold potential we admired over the years—then watched as they suddenly imploded or slowly dissolved, forced to fold, never to be heard from again. If only they (and we!) had had Reginald Nelson's terrific guide to start off on the right foot.

This excellent how-to is a necessity for anyone out there crazy and brave enough to start a theater company. It's an essential, practical, candid, inspiring, informative, and thoroughly entertaining manual.

I had the privilege of directing Reg in our company's production of Studs Terkel's book *Race: How Blacks and Whites Think and Feel About the American Obsession*, and let me just say he's one of the finest actors I've ever known. What's fantastic about Reg (and you can feel it in his writing) is his confidence, tenacity, passion, generosity, talent, and intelligence—each of which is absolutely essential to the success of a theater company. If you possess these same attributes, then this book—and a little luck—are all you need.

DAVID SCHWIMMER

INTRODUCTION

Why open a theater company? Simple: so you can work. Every year, thousands of young people receive bachelor of arts or bachelor of fine arts degrees in acting from more than 200 American colleges and universities. There's even been an increase in young actors moving on to receive their master of fine arts degrees from graduate theater programs as well. I have a BFA from Howard University in Washington, D.C., and an MFA from the University of Illinois at Urbana-Champaign. By the time an actor leaves a program and attempts to gain employment at an established theater, he or she has to wait behind a long list of alumni of that particular theater and pray that he or she serves the company's casting needs. Trust me, nothing's worse than salivating year after year over the hope that, at some point in its season, the Public, Guthrie, Goodman, Old Globe, or Steppenwolf produces a play that you *might* be right for. If steady, inspiring work is what you're looking for, your best bet is to round up a posse of peers and do work that speaks to you (and, more important, to an audience). For those of you who want to live your dream of being on the stage, opening your own company is the way to go.

That's exactly what I and a group of friends from undergraduate and graduate school did when we launched Congo Square Theatre Company in the great city of Chicago in the fall of 2000. I was fortunate enough to have attended school with some very talented people, and it seemed natural for all of us to continue working together. The best thing a young artist can do is create his or her own aesthetic, and established organizations have little patience for green actors who are still trying to find themselves. Major theaters spend big money on their productions, and they have a very limited margin of error to waste on an inexperienced actor. If you're going to fall on your face in the beginning of your career, it's best to do it in front of 60 seats instead of 600.

I wrote this book to give you a shot at living your dream of becoming a professional performer. As the founding board president and former managing director of Congo Square, I know firsthand what it takes to lift a theater company off the ground. The book is a business plan for actors by an actor; it's intended to give you the play-by-play on how to attack your theater endeavor with vision, integrity, and passion. In these pages you'll find advice on which jobs offer the most flexibility and how to set up a corporation, develop a board of directors, and choose a mission statement. Finally, you'll learn what it's like to manage an organization as I take you through the highs and lows of the first three seasons of Congo Square, including a high-profile collaboration with the renowned Steppenwolf Theatre Company.

In the five years I was there running the company, we went from a $15,000-a-year organization to a $200,000-a-year operation—complete with two full-time staff members, two part-time assistants, and a large, permanent, fully equipped office. From the outset, those were my goals as a founder: to raise enough funds to sustain the theater, to provide paid positions, and to create community awareness of the company in a short period of time so I would no longer have to work as an administrator but could focus solely on acting instead. In other words, my goal was to establish a stable, professional company and work within it.

The most common reasons that new theater companies fold are a lack of serious artistic focus and fiscal mismanagement. This book discusses ways in which to clear those initial hurdles so your company can achieve the ultimate goal—longevity. Once your enterprise produces three full seasons of plays, the organization should have acquired a blueprint for durability.

All theater needs to exist is space, an audience, and performers. Developing a theater *company*, on the other hand, needs capital, vision, teamwork, passion, organization, tenacity, solid management, and more than a little luck. The journey should be charted only by the courageous, disciplined, and selfless. But for those who can stay the course, it's a journey that offers rich rewards.

HOW TO START YOUR OWN
THEATER COMPANY

SURVIVAL

Employment, Benefits, and Supporting Yourself

If you are a young aspiring actor and you would like to form your own ensemble, the smartest thing you can do in order to achieve your goal is to find a flexible job that allows you to pay for the basics of living while you pursue your dream. A nine-to-five job is the last thing a young artist fresh out of training from a reputable school or conservatory would like to discuss, but it's best to approach your career not only with enthusiasm but also with strategy. You will have enough stress dealing with marketing, finding a rehearsal space, raising money, etc. without having to worry about whether you can afford food and shelter. Unless you're fortunate enough to have a trust fund waiting for you upon graduation, welcome to the real world, kiddo!

Most actors, writers, artists, and musicians pay the bills while pursuing their art by getting jobs in some sector of the service industry. Gigs such as waiting tables, bartending, walking dogs, and the like are relatively plentiful, and they tend to offer flexibility in terms of work schedules. Some offer excellent opportunities to encounter a wide variety of people who have the potential of becoming patrons of your new company; others, such as substitute teaching, can be fulfilling in ways that have nothing to do with money. Each "day job" has its own perks and drawbacks, and finding the one that suits you best can only be accomplished through trial and error as you figure out which one fits your personality and schedule while providing enough money for you to cover your rent, car payments, student loans, and other financial obligations.

Don't Forget About Health Insurance

Health care is expensive in this country, and it's not something to be taken lightly. When you're just starting out in your theater career, you won't qualify for the health care benefits offered by Actors' Equity or the Screen Actors Guild. Your physical and psychological well-being is imperative to your success as an actor and as the cofounder of a theater company. Much like the bodies of dancers and professional athletes, our bodies are our instruments, and they must be well conditioned in order for us to earn a living and to create art. Instead of grabbing the day job that pays the most money, many young artists are willing to cut living expenses to the bone and share cramped apartments with two or more roommates in order to survive on low-paying jobs that offer good health benefits.

Serving Jobs

Serving or waiting tables is something that 90 percent of all struggling actors do at some point to pay the bills as they pursue their dreams. A job as a server offers a steady source of cash, mainly in the form of tips, and great flexibility: if you need a night off to strike a set, catch a preview, or audition for a role, you can simply request it off or trade a shift with a coworker. In addition, some restaurants—especially corporate "theme" restaurants and fine-dining establishments—offer health insurance benefits to full-time employees. Now, I know what you're thinking: "If I'm a professional actor, how can I work full time at another job?" Don't be alarmed. In the restaurant world, full time generally means about 30 hours a week. A nice server shift at a well-managed enterprise shouldn't last more than six hours, leaving you plenty of time in your day to focus on your company.

Whether you find work as a server at a theme restaurant, a fine-dining place, or a greasy spoon depends in large part on your experience in the industry and on your knowledge of food (and, in some cases, wine). The classier the joint, the better the tips. If you're still in school, consider getting a summer entry-level job in an upscale dining establishment where you can learn the ropes without having to worry about paying off that student loan just yet. Even if you're out of school, it's worth considering taking a "lesser" job, such as busboy, at a better restaurant and working your way up to server. My first restaurant job was as a busboy at Planet Hollywood in Chicago. It wasn't the most glamorous or best-paying day gig, but it got my foot in the door at a good place—and after only a month of busing tables, I was promoted to server and started making the "big bucks." After working at Plant Hollywood I took a job as a server at ESPN

Zone (another corporate theme restaurant), where I eventually got several other Congo Square cofounders jobs as well. Theme restaurants can be fun, fast-paced places to work. Full-time employees often receive health insurance, and a server can make between $100 and $150 in tips each night.

Ultimately, though, the goal of any aspiring actor working in the food service industry should be to land a job in a fine-dining restaurant, where it's not uncommon to bring home $250 to $400 in tips a night! In the last two decades, the concept of the celebrity chef has soared in this country (in France, chefs have been treated like royalty since the end of World War II), and the result is many more high-end restaurants in theater towns such as New York, Chicago, and San Francisco— all cities in which people take their dining experiences almost as seriously as they take their drama. Competition for serving jobs in high-end restaurants is fierce, and the jobs themselves can be stressful—often, the server is sandwiched between an incredibly demanding chef and equally demanding guests— but the pay and benefits are considerable, and you don't need to take the job home with you at the end of your shift. Remember, you want to make the most amount of money in the least amount of time so you can devote yourself to your art.

Event and Catering Jobs

Some people just don't want to be tied down to a routine; they would much rather land a day gig that offers only sporadic employment. If you prefer this lifestyle and can handle the uneven cash flow it provides, I recommend you look into catering jobs. Catering is a great way for you to make quick and easy money on an occasional basis. Classified ad Web sites such as craigslist are usually full of notices from companies looking for servers, bartenders, and others to work special events. Such jobs can involve setting up tables or chairs, stocking alcohol, or passing out appetizers or drinks. The downsides are that the work isn't steady—you could be called in to work from the same company five days in a row and then not hear from them for a whole month—and health insurance is almost never offered.

Promotional Jobs

Many advertising and marketing firms hire young, hip people to give away their product to the public. Many of my actor friends have done promotional work, from handing out cigarettes in nightclubs to giving away bottled water or free gum to passersby on street corners. Like catering jobs, promotional gigs can be sporadic, and some of the uniforms or costumes the advertisers have their workers wear can be downright humiliating, but the hourly wage is usually pretty good.

Pet Caretaking and House Sitting Jobs

In Los Angeles, where I currently reside, it seems as though almost everyone has a pet and no one has the time to take care of it. The result is a steady stream of people who are hiring others to walk their dogs, look after their cats, feed their birds and their fish, etc. It's a total dream gig for a struggling actor who also happens to like animals. There are actors in New York who will ask doormen in Manhattan high-rises if any residents need a dog walker. Most people will pay handsomely for the peace of mind that comes with knowing their pets are being well taken care of.

Unlike pet caretaking, house sitting does not tend to offer much in the way of income—but it can offer a great opportunity to save money on rent. House sitting gigs usually involve living in someone's home and taking care of the property, plants, and pets while that person is away for an extended period of time. Such work often comes about as a result of personal referrals, so if house sitting sounds appealing to you, spread the word to your friends and colleagues that you're interested in doing the job.

Personal Training Jobs

Do you like working out and practicing a healthy lifestyle? Would you enjoy helping others achieve their health-related goals? If so, personal training may be a great day gig for you. This is a growing industry, and many organizations offer certification in personal training online. For as little as $300, you can complete a two- to six-week online course and receive certification in one of several disciplines of personal training, including aerobics, self-defense, sports nutrition, and others. Once you receive your certification, you can begin your "career" as a personal trainer by either freelancing or working as an employee at a gym or health club. Steady employment at a company offers a reliable source of income (and, sometimes, health insurance benefits), but personal trainers who work on a freelance basis can charge $50 an hour or more for their services—more than enough to pay for their own health insurance if they develop a solid clientele. When we were getting Congo Square off the ground, one of our ensemble members, Monifa Days, was also working as a certified personal trainer. While most of us were scraping by at our restaurant jobs, she was making good money—and staying in great shape.

Bartending Jobs

Bartending can be a fast-paced and complicated job, depending on the clientele and the types of drinks that are requested. To do the job well, a bartender must have a solid knowledge of the art of mixing cocktails. Those with no experience may find it necessary to take a course in bartending; many such courses offer certification that verifies the graduate knows how to make at least the standard drinks. And most people begin their bartending "careers" by working as a bar back for a couple of months before being promoted to bartender. A bar back makes sure that the bartender has everything required to do his or her job at the moment, and it involves everything from preparing fruit garnishes for cocktails and washing glasses to maintaining the storage room.

Depending on the establishment, bartenders usually make more money than servers, because not only do they receive tips from their bar clients, but they also get a small percentage of each server's tips for making the drinks that have been served in the restaurant that shift. In general, customers treat bartenders with a bit more respect than they do servers, and good bartenders develop their own "clientele" of regulars. The more people who return to the bar because of your skills or personality, the more money you'll make in the form of tips—and the more opportunity you'll have to tell your guests about your theater company. Now, I'm not advocating that you solicit people while you're on someone else's clock—but once guests take a genuine interest in you and your life, why not explain to them what you're trying to accomplish outside work? They may be interested in helping you, possibly in ways you never thought of. Back in my old restaurant days at ESPN Zone, I once met a prominent businessman who ended up helping me recruit board members for Congo Square. Talk about a profitable night's work!

Barista Jobs

Like bartenders, baristas create drinks that can range from the simple to the ridiculously complicated—but instead of pouring booze, baristas deal in coffee. Thanks to the explosion of Starbucks and other such establishments, there is ample opportunity to pick up a job as a barista. The work is often even faster-paced than bartending—especially in the mornings, when people are rushing in to grab a beverage before heading to work.

Although baristas do make some tips, their total income is less—a lot less—than that of a server or a bartender. The one thing employment at a major coffee chain, such as Starbucks, usually has going for it is health insurance. Some coffeehouses even provide full coverage for employees who work as little as 20 hours a week. Like bartending, working as a barista also allows you ample opportunity to establish a rapport with customers who may, in some shape or form, be able to help you with your company—from sitting on the board of directors to attending your first performance.

Temporary Jobs

Some actors have no interest in working in the service industry; instead, they prefer to work in an office environment. Many such actors sign up with temp agencies. These organizations place workers, on a temporary basis, with employers who need help with various office projects. Most agencies require job seekers to take a typing or computer literacy test. The faster and more accurately you can type or the more skilled you are at using Excel, PowerPoint, QuickBooks, and other commonly used computer programs, the higher your pay rate will be. Unfortunately, few temp workers receive health benefits from either the agencies they're signed with or the businesses that use their services.

Substitute Teaching Jobs

This is probably the hardest and most rewarding job an actor can perform while building his or her own company. If you enjoy working with kids and you don't need steady employment in order to survive, substitute teaching might be perfect for you. In most cases, substitute teachers are required to have at least one college degree, and they must pass a state competency test. While you may be able to choose which grade levels you are willing to take on, it's likely that you will find yourself traveling quite a bit to reach a school in need of your services on any given day. As a substitute teacher, you may fill in for a teacher for a day, a week, or more—or you may sit by the phone for days without getting a single call to work. Keep in mind, too, that public schools do not offer health benefits to substitute teachers.

For many people, these drawbacks rule out substitute teaching as a source of financial support. Still, many young actors find that working with children is its own reward. If you're one of these fine people, contact your local school system to find out how to become a substitute teacher in your area.

TALK-BACK NOTES

- Don't let your enthusiasm for the theater blind you to the need for a day gig. Seek out one of the many jobs in the service industry and elsewhere that allow you to pay your basic living expenses while giving you the time and flexibility you need to establish your theater company.

- If you're still in school, get some service experience under your belt before you head out into the unforgiving world. Try to secure an entry-level position at a fine-dining establishment, and learn everything about the business that you can while you're there. Your experience will help you land a better-quality gig once you're out on your own.

- Remember: as an actor, your body is your instrument—so it would behoove you to make sure you can afford to keep it in good shape by getting a job that provides health insurance (or that pays enough for you to get insurance on your own).

2

URGENCY

Passion, Community, and Location

Now that you have settled into a secure and flexible job—one that pays well and that enables you to have some form of health insurance—let's talk about the reason you want to open a theater company. The core motivation for most artists, regardless of the medium in which they work, is expression. Human beings have an almost primal need to express themselves—in relationships, in sports, and, of course, in artistic endeavors. I mentioned in the introduction that actors form theater companies simply so they can work. That is indeed true, but there must also be passion, a burning desire to tell stories that *must* be told. You must possess in your heart the absolute will to execute productions that no other troupe can perform, and the plays you produce should always be relevant, in some shape or form, to current, 21st-century society. The last thing the world needs is another "museum theater" company. The modern stage is currently engaged in an epic battle for audiences and awareness. In order to attract new patrons, today's theaters must compete not only with films and television programs but also with video games, the Internet, and other technology-driven diversions. Theater is also highly susceptible to the economy—more so, even, than many other businesses—because the modern public generally views the performing arts as a luxury, not as a necessity.

Your new theater company must, in many ways, speak to the essence of why people attend theater in the first place. What is it about the art form that separates it from other mediums? Why, despite what seems like a lack of support from the general public, is the theater still here? Why hasn't it gone the way of the dodo bird? The answer may lie in our need for community. Human beings have always felt a yearning to express themselves—to communicate new ideas as well as challenge old ones. The theater is the ultimate medium through which an audience can receive an artist's pure intention, free from government—or, worse, corporate—censorship.

Twenty-first century audiences are much more sophisticated than Hollywood or Madison Avenue realizes. As a result, your commitment has to be unquestionable, your passion beyond measure, in order for your new company to stand a chance of pulling people away from their Facebook page or the latest bestselling novel. Why are you performing this particular play at this particular time, and why should the people in this neighborhood—the audience—care?

Once you answer these questions as an artist, you can then answer them as a businessperson. In fact, if your ensemble can't answer these questions every single season, your company has little chance of succeeding.

Commercial Theaters

In business terms, there are currently two forms of theater produced in the United States today: commercial theater and nonprofit theater. First up for examination is commercial theater, which includes Broadway shows, dinner theater, and most touring company productions. Traditional commercial theater can be extremely expensive to produce because productions are usually large, but the results can be lucrative if a producer invests in the right horse, such as a *Lion King* or a *Ragtime*. The finances of this type of theater are geared much like those of a Hollywood production, with investors keeping a careful eye on the box office and choosing shows (mostly musicals) that they believe will sell. It's safe to say that commercial theater producers aren't interested in artistic vision as much as in entertainment that will appeal to a mass audience. Unless you're fortunate enough to know someone who's already a commercial producer—or, better yet, you own enough capital yourself to become a player in this game—you, like most young actors starting up their own companies, will most likely take the nonprofit theater route instead.

Nonprofit Theaters

The second form of theater being produced in America is the nonprofit venture. A nonprofit organization works to serve the public interest rather than to accumulate profits for the investors and owners. This does not mean that people who work for a nonprofit theater are not paid. Instead, it means that most of the theater's earned income (box office, merchandise, and concessions) should be filtered back into the organization in order for it to maintain operations. Nonprofit theaters are scattered all across the country from Boston to San Diego. They employ the most artists and designers because there are more of them than there are commercial theaters, and they usually stand as pillars in their communities, offering education and outreach programs, student matinees, study guides, and, usually, cheaper ticket prices than commercial theaters.

Congo Square was formed as a nonprofit, which allowed us more room for error and more artistic freedom than we would have enjoyed if we had brought in private investors to start a commercial enterprise. In place of private investors, nonprofits turn to donations from the public as well as grants from foundations large and small.

Before launching a nonprofit venture, you need to understand that the organization's responsibility is to serve the community. Because the nonprofit exists to benefit the people of the community, the government agrees to grant it 501(c)(3) tax-exempt status. This means that when raising funds, the organization is eligible to receive larger donations from foundations and individuals looking to receive a tax write-off. The 501(c)(3) status is essential when you're trying to raise large amounts of capital. You can still raise money without tax-exempt status, but people are generally hesitant to give large sums to such organizations, because they can't claim the donations as tax write-offs. Another great benefit about tax-exempt status is that purchases made on behalf of the theater company (computers, costumes, postcards, etc.) aren't taxed, provided the purchaser shows the merchant the organization's award letter or file number from the IRS. If you need help securing your company's tax-exempt status, contact an organization that specializes in such matters, such as Lawyers for the Creative Arts (www.law-arts.org). I'll discuss LCA in more detail in chapter 4.

"Community theater" should not be considered a pejorative term. Oftentimes when people think of community theater, they picture amateur actors running around the stage in a badly produced church play on Easter Sunday. But most regional theaters—large and small, old and new—run under the banner of "community theater" and serve a much-needed function in our society. By granting nonprofit status to an entity—a museum, a school, a hospital, or a theater—federal and local governments recognize the need to help these organizations survive in this competitive free-enterprise world.

As the founder of a theater company, you have a very serious responsibility to honor that agreement with the government and your patrons. The income you receive from grants and donations will not be taxed, and the people who give those grants and donations to you can receive a break from the government on *their* income taxes. To put it simply, your theater company is a charity, and that's why people donate to it. If the patrons like the work you're producing and you practice sensible fiscal management, you'll not only survive but also thrive. As with any venture, if you're not producing good work and you don't know how to manage your finances, you'll fail.

It's extremely important to be realistic and acknowledge that you probably won't become rich by opening a theater company. Actually, I should say you won't become *financially* rich. You will, however, become very rich in terms of your spiritual and artistic fulfillment. Maybe, if you're lucky, you'll even receive local recognition as a leader in the civic and arts communities. However, it is unlikely you will become wealthy, particularly in the start-up stages of your organization. There are many men and women who make comfortable livings running large theater companies, but usually those organizations have been around for a long time and are blessed with endowments and large numbers of patron subscribers. Your goal is to ultimately get your company into the ranks of such established institutions as the Lookingglass in Chicago, the Manhattan Theatre Club in New York, and the American Conservatory Theater in San Francisco. Each of these legendary troupes started small, built up a fan base, and eventually became pillars in the community. In your case, for the first 10 years, focus on rolling up your sleeves and getting busy. The theater has no room for ego and narcissism; it's simply too difficult a profession to accommodate personal drama. In order to achieve your goal of putting on successful productions year after year, season after season, you need to rely on too many people both artistically and financially to let your own, or anyone else's, ego get in the way of solid work. Most people can smell someone with a personal agenda a mile away—so you'd better be about the *work* and not about yourself.

Location

When I first decided to open up a theater company with Derrick Sanders, an old buddy of mine from my undergraduate years, one of the first things we needed to decide was "where?" You don't have to be Donald Trump to realize that location, location, location is the key to any successful business. Even something as lucrative as McDonald's would fail if it opened in the wrong area. As a couple of young African American actors with astronomical ambitions, we had very particular needs. We were all too aware that the theater had become a middle- to upper-class pastime, and we wanted to be in a town that had a large African American population that would patronize our business. That town turned out to be Chicago.

Why We Chose Chicago

When A. J. Liebling, a journalist for the *New Yorker* magazine, called Chicago "the Second City" in 1952, he meant it as a pejorative term, implying that New York City was number one and Chicago a distant runner-up when it came to restaurants, bars, nightclubs, art museums, and, of course, the theater. Little did he realize his insult would be taken up as a clarion call by a theatrical movement the likes of which the country had never before witnessed. The Second City, the famed comedy improvisational troupe, opened its doors in Chicago in 1959, at the beginning of the city's grassroots theater movement, and hit its full stride during the 1970s. A host of other Chicago theaters came along at that time, giving birth to what was soon becoming a renaissance for American theater. Derrick and I researched this tradition of start-up theaters and learned not only that Chicago was supportive of them but also that the city's home-grown theaters had launched the careers of playwrights, actors, and directors who would go on to win virtually every award the industry had to offer. There was the Organic Theater Company, which produced the debut of David Mamet's *Sexual Perversity in Chicago*. Afterward, Mamet formed his own company, called the St. Nicholas Theatre Company, with actor William H. Macy. Victory Gardens, Defiant Theatre, Redmoon, Court Theatre, the Shakespeare Repertory (which would eventually become the Chicago Shakespeare Theater and find a new home on the city's Navy Pier), Famous Door, and a group of Northwestern alumni who called their organization the Lookingglass Theatre Company—all started in this town and provided us with examples to strive for. Perhaps no American theater ensemble influenced young actors more than Chicago's own Steppenwolf Theatre Company, the legendary "rock 'n' roll" troupe that was begun in a suburban church basement.

When I was in my final year of graduate school, theater veteran Chuck Smith, an acclaimed stage director and resident artist at Chicago's Goodman Theatre and a professor at Columbia College Chicago, opened my eyes to the opportunity that existed in the city where I was born. I'd come back to Chicago to audition for Chuck, who was directing a production of August Wilson's *Ma Rainey's Black Bottom* for the Goodman. Chuck was proud of the fact that, at the time, Chicago was the only city in the country with five African American theater companies: eta Creative Arts, the Chicago Theatre Company, the Black Ensemble Theater, the Onyx Theatre Ensemble of Chicago, and MPAACT. I was impressed that the city was able to support more than one or two African American theaters. No other city—not New York City; not Atlanta; not even Washington, D.C.—had five black companies that offered full seasons to their patrons year after year. I left the meeting amazed—and convinced that our new company had to be in Chicago. The fact that the city could support five African American theater companies indicated two very important facts: first, that blacks patronized theater in that town; second, that whites *also* patronized African American theater in Chicago. And I knew that if Chicago could sustain five African American theater groups, it could probably support six.

Chicago's Legacy of Great African American Theater

Located near the South Shore neighborhood of Chicago's South Side, eta Creative Arts is the oldest and largest of the black companies in the city. Founded by the fiery, outspoken elder of the community, Abena Joan P. Brown, in 1971 and led by artistic director Runako Jahi, the company is a non-Equity theater, which means it does not run under Actor's

Equity union contracts—and, therefore, the pay for actors and stage managers isn't the greatest—but it is very much respected in the city and it offers wonderful programming for children and adults.

The Chicago Theatre Company, which was cofounded by Chuck Smith in 1984, was an Equity theater house that offered professional black actors great opportunities to do serious work. Sadly, the Chicago Theatre Company closed its doors in 2006.

The Black Ensemble Theater, another Equity house, was founded in 1976 by producer, playwright, and actress Jackie Taylor. Specializing in musical biographies of African Americans, the organization, which is located in the Uptown neighborhood of Chicago's North Side, produces hit show after hit show about such legendary performers as R&B vocalist Jackie Wilson, blues legend Howlin' Wolf, and many others.

MPAACT (the MAAT Production Association of Afrikan Centered Theatre) was started in 1990 by a group of student activists at the University of Illinois at Urbana-Champaign. Two years later they moved the company to Chicago, where today its mission remains focused on creating new works and collaborative art. MPAACT ensemble members take pride in producing new material, as well as in the fact that they're a company not only of actors but also of directors, sound and lightning designers, photographers, and more.

The short-lived Onyx Theatre Ensemble of Chicago was founded in 1994 by director and actor Ron OJ Parson, who also served as the company's artistic director, and Alfred Wilson. In 1998 the company won great acclaim for its coproduction, with the Goodman Theatre, of *Let Me Live*, which won a Jeff Award (Chicago's version of a Tony Award) for best ensemble.

When you're selecting a location for your company, it's important to remember that you don't want to try to reinvent the wheel. It's best to start in a place where there is already an infrastructure to support the type of theater you want to produce. It doesn't have to be in a major metropolis; it just needs to be an area that has an established capacity and willingness to support art.

Mentors, Advisory Boards, and Legitimacy

Any successful organization, whether it's a Fortune 500 corporation or local small business, has to rely on trustworthy experts who sign on to the venture. That's why your next step as the founder is to recruit advisors. Look for veterans of the theater who are acutely familiar with the game you're about to play. Don't be shy about approaching these pros for advice. Many people who are established in their careers don't mind giving guidance if they sense hunger, passion, and sincerity.

Chuck Smith was there for us from the very beginning, and only a couple years after we formed the ensemble, he would direct some of our best shows. He thrived in the role of mentor, and we thrived under his guidance. Another well-established theater veteran who advised us at the beginning was the late, great playwright August Wilson. My cofounder Derrick, who would later become our artistic director, had run into Mr. Wilson at an international arts festival in Grahamstown, South Africa. After listening to the playwright speak, Derrick boldly asked him out for coffee. Mr. Wilson accepted, and that's when Derrick told him about our plans to open a theater company. The two kept in contact, and a couple of years later, not only did Mr. Wilson's *The Piano Lesson* serve as our organization's inaugural production, but August Wilson (a true man of his word) even attended the closing night performance. Derrick had taken a risk by approaching a theater icon, and it paid off in the form of a rewarding, years-long relationship with our young company.

When you find professionals who agree to offer guidance, see if they'll go one step further and sit on your advisory board. This doesn't really cost them any money or additional time (certainly not the amount of time a regular board member will devote to the organization)—just the lending of their good names to a just cause. Advisory board members come from various professional backgrounds and should be established leaders in their chosen fields. They don't have to be theater professionals, but instead can come from all walks of life. They might be lawyers, accountants, or any other high-profile professionals who can't give a full-time commitment to the company like the "traditional" board member does. Serving as advisors, they can help answer the many questions that arise with the launch of any business endeavor. While they can't assist you in the "heavy lifting" of a start-up organization, the goal is to get them involved enough so that they eventually join the actual board of directors.

One way to get people involved as advisory members is simply to invite them to a fundraiser for the company or to the opening-night gala of a production. In the initial stages of establishing your organization, a civic leader appearing at your event can boost the entire ensemble's morale as well as add glamour, authenticity, and credibility to your company.

Your mentors and advisory board will prove invaluable as you begin recruiting regular board members and raising money. When Chuck Smith and August Wilson agreed to serve on our advisory board, it gave us legitimacy. Without them, we would not have been nearly as successful as we were at recruiting our board of directors and keeping our organization running during the first few years.

Choosing a Neighborhood

Once you have decided on the city or town you'd like to be based in and have spoken to and signed on a few advisors, it's time to zero in on the specific section of town you want to be associated with. Most large cities, and even many smaller ones, are made up of a large number of neighborhoods, each with its own energy and demographic. On the North Side of Chicago, for example, is a section called Andersonville. The community is home to many LGBT (lesbian, gay, bisexual, and transgender) residents—so it should come as no surprise that it is the headquarters of About Face Theatre, which produces LGBT-themed plays. In Hyde Park, Chicago's South Side neighborhood that is home to the University of Chicago, Court Theatre caters to the neighborhood's highly intellectual residents by producing classical theater. It is extremely important to tap into the energy of the neighborhood that best represents your target market, since residents living near the theater will be your initial audience members. A small theater company in the right location often acts as a "mom and pop" shop that the locals take special pride in patronizing. Neighborhoods come and go, of course, so it's best to find one that's up-and-coming so your company can benefit from the city's investment in that vibrant new community. Your theater company should be specifically designed to help galvanize that neighborhood.

It also helps to know the history of the town you're gong to plant your roots in. Due to the wealth of artists in Chicago theater, I was able to constantly continue my education by speaking with and interviewing older actors whenever I found myself cast in a play with them. I relished listening to old stories about the early days of how, for example, the Chicago Shakespeare Theater began its first production on the roof of a pub. These veteran thespians offered wonderful insight and hope to a struggling young actor.

When we were researching Chicago neighborhoods in which to plant our roots, I realized that the Near West Side was a changing community that was quickly being gentrified and that would soon need a theater company. It already had many of the city's best restaurants, and the young professionals moving there loved the nightlife. Back when I was born in that part of town in the early 1970s, it was known as a ghetto and was home to the Henry Horner Homes housing projects. Now realtors called the area "West Haven." Our timing couldn't have been better, and we fit that neighborhood like a glove. Residents of that community had no theater to call their own until we arrived, and our young, diverse population of new neighbors were quick to embrace us and patronize our company.

Creating Community Liaisons

Once you've selected the neighborhood in which to set up shop, immediately ally yourself with the merchants in the area. Consider giving the owners of local stores, restaurants, and bars complimentary tickets to your productions so they can talk up your company. Negotiate special ticket offers to residents and apartment managers in the area as a way of introducing yourself to the neighborhood. During your first season you're going to be giving away a lot of tickets just for the sake of public relations, so make the most of the opportunity to get your community interested and involved in your efforts. And, if possible, support neighborhood businesses as well by purchasing printing, graphic design work, advertising, concessions, and so forth from local shops and service companies.

TALK-BACK NOTES

- Before you seek donations, grants, or other funds for your new nonprofit theater company, secure 501(c)(3) tax-exempt status through the IRS. Big foundations and deep-pocketed donors usually require documentation that your company is tax exempt, as they will want to use their donations as tax write-offs.

- By building a respected advisory board, you establish a support system you can rely on for advice and other resources, and create a reputation as a serious-minded organization.

- The key to launching a successful theater company, or any business, is finding the right location—not just the right city but also the right neighborhood within that city. Look for a community of people whose energy, culture, and interests seem a good fit for the type of theater you want to produce.

3

PURPOSE

Name, Logo, and
Mission Statement

Theater is all about a leap of faith. When you're tired or frustrated—as happens in any job, but in the arts, the ups and downs can be even more dramatic—you and your peers can draw inspiration from the meaning behind the organization's name and the mission of the theater. The challenges confronting the theater company you and your comrades build will most certainly seem overwhelming, even insurmountable, at times. You must always remember your higher goals and the value you're bringing to the community, whether it's via a thought-provoking new piece on the death penalty or through the educational program you offer to kids.

Set tangible, well-considered goals and objectives. What do you hope to accomplish in your first season or with your first production? Would you like to receive rave reviews and sell out every night, or are you much more interested in mounting a modest production of experimental work by a new playwright? Whatever the case may be, you and your comrades must be crystal clear about your objectives before heading into preproduction—and fully committed to doing whatever it takes to achieve them. Once you're frustrated in the heat of battle (fundraising, designer meetings, marketing, etc.), it's easy to forget why you formed the company in the first place. Time and time again, everyone in your ensemble will face tests of their passion and commitment—not just to acting but also to building a company.

Create a Brand Name

You've consulted with your advisors or mentors, established an advisory board, and decided what city and neighborhood to settle in. Now comes the fun part: what are you going to call yourself? I strongly believe that names should have meaning— that they should define who you are before anyone ever lays eyes on one of your productions. Your company's name is its calling card in a cluttered market, and it must separate your theater from all the rest.

In my opinion, the best name is one that encapsulates and defines a theater company's mission. Focus on coming up with a name that is instantly recognizable, powerful, intriguing, and just a wee bit mysterious—it's a statement of how you view your company and what separates you from your competition.

For a start-up theater company, the name must inspire not only the ensemble but also the community at large. Your company's name clues the neighborhood, the city, and the future patrons of your theater into who you are and what you're trying to do. At this point in your venture, you should have a general idea of the types of plays you'd like to produce. Use that information to help you narrow your choices of a name for the company. You can also try brainstorming, listing names of other theater companies whose missions are similar to yours, and doing online research of historical events and movements. Be open to receiving inspiration from the world around you. It might come from music, movies, art installations, novels, fashion trends, social media—even video games. If a name inspires you, it will probably inspire the public.

I came up with the name Congo Square while reading an excellent mystery novel by Barbara Hambly titled *A Free Man of Color*. Set in early 19th-century New Orleans, it deals with a free black musician who is accused of murder. In one dark, brilliant scene, the police sergeant questions the musician, asking him, "What were you doing walking through Congo Square at that time of night?" It hit me right then and there— Congo Square! Historic Congo Square is located just north of the French Quarter in New Orleans. In the 18th and 19th centuries, slaves and free blacks would gather in the square on Sundays to dance, sing, play music, and perform. Many of the different African tribes could communicate only through the drum, and in Congo Square they created music using both their native African instruments and European instruments such as the violin. Historians believe that's how jazz was born. People always had a visceral response whenever I mentioned Congo Square as a possible moniker, and the name certainly reflected the type of work we wanted to do: theater from the African diaspora. With a name that evoked such a rich cultural legacy, we were well on our way to creating the "buzz" a start-up theater company desperately needs to get noticed.

You want the name of your theater company to have that kind of effect on people. Remember, we are in the culture business, and many folks pay top dollar just to live near culture and entertainment. Your job as the founder is to offer them high-quality, "buzz-worthy" culture and entertainment—even if, while you're getting established, you have to keep ticket prices low.

Your Logo

Believe it or not, there's a method to the madness of every rap song in which the artist's record label is mentioned a thousand times throughout the hook. The producer of that song is promoting the record label brand as much as, if not more than, he or she is promoting the artist. The idea is to instill the impression that if you like this particular artist on the label, you'll probably *love* the next artist on the same label. You need to figure out how to do the same with your theater, and one way is through your logo.

As you're thinking of your company's name, visualize it in the form of a logo. Once you have an idea of what you want, the next step is to get the logo produced. You can accomplish this at minimal cost via several methods.

- Find a graphic design student who is interested in adding to his or her portfolio at little or no cost to you. Together, hammer out a killer image. It's a win-win for both parties. You can approach the art department of your alma mater or of a local college or community college to find out if a student would be interested, or put up ads on the department bulletin board.
- Find out if there is an arts organization in your area that provides services to members at a discount.
- Hold a contest, and award the person who creates the winning design two tickets to the company's first show.

Regardless of how you have your logo created, be sure to get a signed, written agreement that grants you all rights, including sole copyright, to the logo in perpetuity.

This all may seem like you're putting the cart before the horse, but remember, you're laying the groundwork for the future success of your organization. When you introduce yourself to the city, every detail must be in place—and in order for that to happen, you need to have considered and made a conscious choice about every aspect of the company.

I'll never forget a patron's comment after seeing a performance of our first production, *The Piano Lesson*: "Man, you guys have come out on the scene as if you've been here all the time!" That's *exactly* the type of response you want from audiences and philanthropists. If you present yourself with competence and confidence, your theater company will soon be branded in the community's psyche, and you'll be well on your way to running a sustainable organization.

What's the Buzz?

Before we were even close to producing our first show, we sold Congo Square Theatre Company T-shirts. Why? Because we were creating buzz and building a brand that we wanted people to anticipate. The ultimate brand in Chicago theater is the Steppenwolf Theatre Company. While the theater's founders took the name from the title of a novel by Hermann Hesse, the fact that it was also the name of a popular rock 'n' roll band reflected the brash energy of the troupe and helped to generate hype about them. Today, the Steppenwolf brand is recognized throughout the American theater scene, and the ensemble's acting style has influenced countless Chicago troupes over the years. The company is even able to offer acting classes in Chicago and Los Angeles to students around the world, all because they built an awesome brand based on a great name—and even greater art.

Mission Statement

Now comes one of the hardest, and probably most important, parts of forming your own company: crafting the organization's mission statement. The mission statement is your company's Constitution, Bill of Rights, holy Koran, and holy Bible all rolled into one. It's going to define you—to yourselves as an organization and to the general public. Comparing the work that you have accomplished to your mission statement allows you to determine the success or failure of any endeavor—and by using the mission statement as your guide, you can prevent arguments among ensemble members. Remember, the degree to which you stay true to your mission statement affects not only the way in which the critics will judge you but also the way in which you'll judge yourselves.

When creating your mission statement, keep in mind the following.

- Your mission statement should state who you are and the type of work you'll produce
- Each element of the mission statement should carry significant meaning: no superfluous flourishes should be included
- Your mission statement must be easy to understand, and it must set your company apart from competitors in a tangible way

When we started Congo Square, we debated constantly about the mission statement. Finally, in the dead of night at my kitchen table, we all agreed on the following.

Congo Square Theatre Company is an ensemble dedicated to artistic excellence. In producing definitive and transformative theater spawned from the African diaspora, as well as from other world cultures, Congo Square Theatre Company seeks to establish itself as an institution of multicultural theater.

The first message we wanted to impart to the public through our mission statement is that we are an *ensemble*. That was extremely important because we wanted audiences to appreciate the work of the group as a whole instead of focusing on a single actor. It was also important because it helped to reassure everyone in the ensemble that all of their hard work to start up a company wouldn't be in vain—that they were almost guaranteed an opportunity to perform.

Some of the best theater occurs when a cast of performers works in concert to execute a beautifully constructed play. Steppenwolf and, later, Lookingglass Theatre Company both represented the gold standard of Chicago ensemble-based theater, and we looked to them as an example. Their productions and work ethic spoke for themselves, and theirs was the level we wanted to reach. We also looked to the historic roots of New Orleans's Congo Square and to the legacy we were drawing on when we chose that name for our theater. The actors were to be like jazz musicians in a band: each member would play an equal part in the success or failure of the group as a whole. Winning is much more fun with a team—and losing is easier to stomach with loyal comrades by your side. For those reasons if nothing else, it's best to part company quickly with selfish people, because when you receive a setback, those people will instantly reveal their character. In some cases you can use the mission statement to keep egos in check or even ask a member to leave the company.

We intentionally set the bar high: we wanted to produce both new and existing works, and we needed to approach each endeavor as if it were the ultimate, definitive production of a play that people had perhaps seen many times before. In our mind, *definitive* simply meant that we had to be flawless in the execution of the plays we performed. It didn't matter if the Goodman or Victory Gardens had just done a production of *Fences*; our goal was to get across the message "you haven't seen it until you've seen *our* version." This statement was idealistic and borderline arrogant, but that is exactly the attitude you're going to need to get you through your first three seasons. If a company can survive three seasons without going under financially, that usually means you've found an audience.

Another key element of our mission was the intention to *transform* an audience—to shift its current frame of thought into another consciousness. We wanted people who entered our space to be lifted into another time and place. In order to accomplish something of that magnitude, we as actors had to totally commit to the work and transform ourselves—to become whatever the playwright dictated. This was yet another Herculean task we eagerly placed on ourselves.

We also wanted to take black theater to the next level in Chicago. To us, that meant not just doing new works but also mining the black canon of literature, including plays from Africa and the Caribbean. That's how *the African diaspora* became a huge part of our identity. We were able to set ourselves apart with such plays because they were on the cutting edge of black theater at the time. The established black theaters in Chicago rarely did pieces in which actors employed heavy stage dialects. Our ensemble members had received excellent training in dialects, so we were not afraid to tackle difficult dialect work.

Not content to produce only black theater, we wanted ultimately to produce plays or theater from *other world cultures* as well. We all live in this world together, and only through understanding other people can we truly understand ourselves. The more specific a play is, the more universal it is, and a true people's theater is a multicultural institution that accurately reflects our multicultural world. Every theater of color realizes the importance of serving its community by producing works that speak directly to that community, but it's also important to explore other cultures and to expose the audience to new ideas and new works.

More Mission Statements

Here are two examples of really cool mission statements—those of the Manhattan Theatre Club and the Lookingglass Theatre Company.

Manhattan Theatre Club's Mission Statement

To *produce* a season of innovative work with a series of productions as broad and diverse as New York itself.

To *encourage* significant new work by creating an environment in which writers and theatre artists are supported by the finest professionals producing theatre today.

To *nurture* new talent in playwriting, musical composition, directing, acting and design.

To *reach* young audiences with innovative programs in education and maintain a commitment to cultivating the next generation of theatre artists.

Lookingglass Theatre Company's Mission Statement

When Alice walked through the looking glass, she walked into a world beyond imagination. She walked into a world more involving and intoxicating than any movie or circus, more thrilling than a high-speed chase, more frightening than a child's nightmare, and more beautiful than a thunderstorm on a hot summer night. She awoke with a new sense of herself in the world and her own power within it.

Reflected in Lewis Carroll's achievement is the mission of the Lookingglass Theatre Company. Through theatre, which invites, even demands, interaction with its audience, our goal is to fire the imagination with love, to celebrate the human capacity to taste and smell, weep and laugh, create and destroy, and wake up where we first fell—changed, charged and empowered.

The Lookingglass Theatre Company combines a physical and improvisational rehearsal process centered on ensemble with training in theatre, dance, music, and the circus arts. We seek to redefine the limits of theatrical experience and to make theatre exhilarating, inspirational, and accessible to all.

Focus

Once you announce your mission to the world, you mustn't divert from it. If you state that you perform theater from the Irish diaspora, don't turn around and do *The Sea Gull* just because a few ensemble members love Anton Chekhov. Actors can be tough to manage, and many of them will, at some point, want to branch out and try something different from the type of works that your company has produced in the past. This is totally understandable and is to be expected—just make sure that such branching out doesn't lead the company away from its stated mission, and that your organization remains true to what made it successful in the first place.

Like the members of the ensemble, board members, too, may begin to feel confined after a while, and some may lose interest in the company's mission. Raising money on behalf of different charities or nonprofit organizations can be extremely difficult, particularly in a tough economy. Every group, whether it's a museum, a dance troupe, or a theater company, seems to be fighting for the same dollar these days. Some of your board members will undoubtedly serve on other organizations' boards as well, and they may get frustrated by the constant need to raise money. When money is tight, some board members may attempt to "shake things up" in order to secure more funds. That can be a good thing—provided the people on your board believe in the goal and direction of the organization and understand that they serve the company; the company is not there to serve them.

TALK-BACK NOTES

- Your company's name and logo have a long-term intangible effect on the success of your new company. When selecting them, seek the input of all company members and be very deliberate in your choices. If a name inspires you, it will probably inspire the public.

- The mission statement helps to keep your young organization focused. More important, it helps you to establish—and stay true to—your company's goals and vision.

- Once you've established your mission and have announced it to the world, don't allow yourself, other ensemble members, or board members to stray from it.

- It's extremely important for theaters of color to not only serve their communities by producing work that speaks to them, but also to explore other cultures and expose their audiences to new works and ideas.

4

GUIDANCE

Board of Directors
and Legal Assistance
Organizations

Many theater companies fail simply because they don't take the time to lay down the groundwork that ensures they'll have the resources and guidance they need to survive. It takes at least a year to recruit a decent board of directors, raise enough funds to launch the company, and file the correct documents with state and local officials—all things that must be accomplished before you even begin to work on your first production. You want to present your company to the public in as polished and professional a way as possible, and you must be certain that you have the funds you need to see you through at least the start-up stage of your endeavor.

Financial resources aren't the only commodity you're going to need; you must secure human resources, too. Perhaps the most important of these is your board of directors. When your board and the acting ensemble are on the same page in terms of the organization's mission, nothing can stop you. One of the most rewarding things I learned when I founded a non-profit company is that *people invest in people*. Never forget that the individuals who sit on your board are there because they want to be there, not because that have to be. They're there because they believe in you, your vision, and your company's mission, and they should never be taken for granted.

This sounds obvious, but you would be surprised (or perhaps not) at how quickly some artists forget about the board members' contributions once they've received a few good reviews. Always remember that successful theater requires a team effort, and that the artists and the board of directors must work together to create a successful organization. Neither can survive without the other, and both are invaluable resources.

Board of Directors

The board of directors serves as a representative of the public, as a liaison between the company and the community. Its job is to ensure that the organization fulfills its obligations to the community and maintains the integrity of its mission, as expressed in its mission statement, at all times. Board members' specific responsibilities include:

Responsibilities to the Company
- Review and approve the company's annual budget
- Ensure that directors adhere to budgets
- Assist in the development of long-term goals and growth

- Assess the growth of the company and ensure that any changes in its direction, focus, and activities are in compliance with the mission statement
- Prepare and deliver semiannual reviews of the artistic and managing directors
- Approve company fundraising events
- Develop and participate in board fundraising events
- Review laws that pertain to the company and ensure that the company remains in compliance with all such laws

Responsibilities to the Board
- Elect executive officers and committee chairs
- Prepare and deliver semiannual reviews of officers' performances and strategies
- Participate in the development of the board's long-term goals
- Chair or sit on committees
- Prepare and present semiannual assessments of committees' development, strengths, and weaknesses
- Review and approve committee budget reports
- Review laws as they pertain to the board and ensure that the board remains in compliance with all such laws

The most successful boards of directors are composed of diverse groups of professionals, each of whom brings specific strengths to the company. For example, a good five-member board might include two artists, a lawyer, an accountant, and a professional in some other field—I recommend a high-profile restaurateur.

- Artists act as liaisons between the board and the ensemble. They help other board members to understand the delicate creative process under which a theater company must operate, and remind the board of the need to balance commercial considerations with creative risks that foster the artistic development of the ensemble.

- A lawyer assists in creating contracts for the people you hire, setting up the bylaws of the organization, determining the way in which the board functions as a governing body, and in ensuring that both the company and the board are in compliance with all local, state, and federal laws and regulations
- An accountant can assist the managing director in overseeing company finances and can serve as the board treasurer
- A restaurateur can prove invaluable in terms of getting the word out about your new company, and can host fundraising and other company-related events

Not long after we established our Congo Square board of directors, we added Cliff Rome, a world-class chef, to the board. Cliff hosted readings, fundraisers, and other company-related events at his establishment. These activities served to introduce us to his clientele, who not only quickly became our patrons but also spread the word about our new theater company.

My method of finding a restaurateur to sit on our board was pretty straightforward: I walked up and down a busy block in the neighborhood looking for restaurants, bars, merchants, and other potential supporters, and I boldly introduced myself to Cliff. After explaining my plan to open a theater company in the area, I asked if he would be interested in joining our board of directors. To my surprise, he said yes—and just like that, we were a step closer to achieving our goals.

Although it worked out well for us, I can't say that I'd recommend such an informal method of recruiting board members to your theater company. It's best to approach this important task in a more structured way. Here are some basic questions you might want to ask when interviewing prospective board members.

- Why would you like to be a board member of this organization?
- What type of experience have you had that would enhance your contribution as an active board member?
- In which of the following areas do you have experience?
    Financial matters
    Public speaking
    Fundraising
    Marketing
- Are you able and willing to give a three-year commitment to this organization?
- As a board member you will be expected to actively participate in or oversee various tasks and activities. Do you foresee having any problems doing any of the following?
    Advocating for the organization
    Attending board meetings
    Developing and participating in fundraisers
    Working on various committees of the board

Keep in mind that although you will certainly want some board members who are experienced at serving in such a capacity at other organizations, your young company's board of directors may include people who have never before served on a board. That's not a bad thing; sometimes the folks who have no prior experience are the ones who are most willing to work to earn it (and let's face it—at least in the first few years of your company's existence, it's not likely that the CEO of Kraft Foods will be knocking on your door and asking to become a board member). Regardless of his or her experience, however, it's crucial that each prospective board member understands exactly what will be expected of him or her.

During the first couple of years of operation, you may have a revolving door of board members as you—and the people you recruit—figure out the proper mix of seasoned members and inexperienced young professionals. Don't be discouraged; your company will eventually settle on the right combination. The key is to have the artistic director nurture the ensemble while the managing director continues to nurture and inspire the board.

Board Manual

A board manual is an extremely important tool for a young organization. Not only does it demonstrate that you're serious, but it also shows that you've given a great deal of thought to, and have put a lot of effort into, the company. The manual may be shown to the prospective board members you attempt to recruit (it will certainly impress the professional socialite you're trying to woo into your company), and each new board member should be given a copy as soon as you take him or her on.

The board manual should contain copies of important documents, such as the company's bylaws and 501(c)(3) tax exemption documents, as well as information about the individuals involved in the organization. It should also include a document that outlines your company's five-year plan. To create this outline, you'll have to think about such critical subjects as your strategies for audience development, whether or not you want the theater to be an Equity house, how you intend to raise money and generate publicity, and what your plans are for community outreach and education.

Community Outreach and Education

Provided your company has the manpower to do so, it's always great to implement an educational program for the community as part of your organization's efforts. This endeavor can build community awareness of and support for your theater, and it's an excellent way to expose children and others to the arts. Numerous grants are available to fund programs that help children through drama, and these grants can be used to offer livable wages to some of your ensemble members. I strongly recommend that you include a good community arts program as an element of your five-year plan.

Your company board manual should contain the following:

- Theater mission statement
- Articles of incorporation
- 501(c)(3) tax exemption document
- Company bylaws
- Five-year plan of organization
- List of existing board officers, with contact information for each
- CVs of all ensemble and board members
- Minutes of past board meetings

Actors' Equity

Working with Actor's Equity may or may not be your goal during the first five years of your existence. It was important for us at Congo Square because many of us wanted to be able to work at other union houses so that we could secure a livable wage by acting as we pursued our dream of starting our own company.

The decision of whether or not to become an Equity house—and at what point, exactly, it should happen—should be made by the ensemble as a whole. When you decide it's time for your company to make that leap and become a union house, reach out to your regional Actors' Equity office for assistance in making that goal a reality. Remember that different cities and regions are regulated by different union contracts. For example, Chicago has its own contract deal called CAT, or Chicago Area Theatres, while the New England region operates under the NEAT, or New England Area Theatres, contract agreement.

Board Officers

Once you've formed your board of directors, the board should elect the executive officers, who will execute the organization's agenda. Here's a breakdown of who they are and what their responsibilities should be.

President
- Serves as head of the board and oversees its daily operations and development
- Sets work standards for the board and makes sure that the board fulfills its obligations to both the community and the company

- Works with the theater's artistic and managing directors to make sure that the company upholds its mission
- Attends all board functions and provides assistance as needed to board committees
- Serves as the head of all fundraising activities

Vice President

- Prepares budgets for committees
- Reviews and approves all budgets for the theater submitted by the treasurer
- Chairs committees as needed
- Heads all meetings in the event of the president's absence
- Serves as the successor to the president, if necessary, until such time that the board elects a new president

Treasurer

- Serves as chair of the finance committee
- Reviews and approves all budgets for the theater and submits such budgets to the vice president for approval
- Keeps detailed records of trustees' contributions to the organization to ensure that they are being productive and proactive
- Keeps detailed records of funds filtered to theater by various grants and foundations
- Assists with fundraising events
- Ensures that the theater meets all of its financial obligations

Secretary

- Maintains official records of all board meetings
- Prepares and distributes agendas of board meetings

- Takes minutes of all board meetings and distributes them to the other board members
- Chairs committees if needed
- Assists the president in the development of official documents, packets, and literature

This breakdown of roles and responsibilities should be included in the "company bylaws" section of your board manual, along with information on terms of office, officer meetings, and removal of officers. Here is a sample of the language you might include to address those issues.

Term of Office
All executive members shall hold position for a term of three (3) years. Each officer will hold a term until a successor has been elected and qualified. An officer may resign at any time by written notice to the Board of Directors. Resignation is effective upon receipt of notice, unless otherwise stated in the notice. A new officer will then be selected but not take office prior to effective date.

Officer Meetings
Meetings of the officers will be held every six months at the registered office of the theater or at such place or places designated by the president by written notice.

Removal of Officers
As noted in Article 7, Section 7.0 of the Bylaws, any officer may be removed from said position by a majority vote of the Board of Directors at any time.

Payments and Fees

No member of the board of directors can *ever* be paid for the duties he or she performs for the organization. Serving on a board is a voluntary obligation, and experienced board members know that they will not be compensated for this very time-consuming work. Make sure that any prospective board members who have no experience serving in this capacity know that, too—*before* they agree to take on the position.

However, when we recruited our board members, we charged each member an annual board fee. A board fee helps to ensure that a prospective board member takes the position seriously and that he or she is committed to fulfilling the duties associated with it. In addition, board fees assessed during the start-up phase are essential, in that they provide the funds that are needed to pay for immediate operational expenses. We used the board fees we received to help pay for such start-up operational costs as the design and production of business cards and letterhead stationery and the creation of our company Web site.

I recommend that, as a new company, you charge each board member a board fee of no more than $400. As your organization establishes itself and becomes more and more successful, you can assess larger board fees. At the major theater companies across the country, a board fee can easily run into the thousands of dollars.

Checks and Balances

Once your board of directors has been established and has elected its officers, your next step should be to open a company bank account. Use the board fees that you've collected from all the new members as the initial deposit. The signers on the account should be the board treasurer and the theater's managing director, with the managing director being the primary signer, as he or she is responsible for running the day-to-day operations of the organization. A third signer might be either the theater's artistic director or the board president, depending on how your company is organized. All things being equal, I recommend going with the board president in order to bolster the company's financial transparency to funders and the public.

Incorporation and Legal Assistance

Now that you've selected your company name, finalized your mission statement, and established a board of directors, it's finally time to incorporate and make your dream a reality. There are many organizations out there that help start-up companies get off the ground. These organizations can also help with legal issues and concerns. Two such organizations are the Foundation Center (www.foundationcenter.org) and the American Association of Community Theatre (www.aact .org). The Foundation Center's mission is to strengthen the nonprofit sector by advancing knowledge about U.S. philanthropy. It maintains learning centers in New York City, Washington, D.C., San Francisco, Atlanta, and Cleveland. Its Web site is a wonderful resource for those who want to learn how to incorporate a business. The American Association of Community Theatre's aim is to improve communities one theater at a time. Its Web site offers an abundance of resources for start-up companies, including online forums, networking tools, newsletters, and, of course, information on how to incorporate.

A third organization—one on which I relied time and time again—is Lawyers for the Creative Arts, or LCA (www .law-arts.org). I had heard about the group from a friend of mine who lived in New York, and I discovered that it had a Chicago branch. I immediately contacted the organization and asked for help in figuring out what, exactly, I needed to do in order to get started. Since the beginning of time, lawyers have had a bad reputation—but I can truly testify that the generous attorneys at this organization help keep Chicago and other cities thriving as cultural meccas. The man who ran the LCA nonprofit-incorporation clinic I attended was Howard Arnett, a former New York prosecutor. His most important message throughout the entire three-hour seminar was: *Don't play around with the IRS. The government will shut you down in a heartbeat if it thinks for one second you are misappropriating funds.* I received his message loud and clear, and I reiterated it to my colleagues. Remember, even if your company is small and doesn't make much money, the IRS will come after you if it thinks you're not adhering to its regulations.

The most essential service LCA provides nonprofit start-ups is pairing them with large law firms that perform pro bono work. LCA partnered us with Winston & Strawn, an international practice that has offices all over the world. Sean McCumber was the young attorney assigned to file our application for 501(c)(3) tax-exempt status. It just so happened that Sean was a recent graduate of the law school at the University of Illinois, so we were fellow alums. Sean helped us receive our tax-exempt status in a record four months, and off we went.

It's essential that you acquire legal assistance when filing for your tax-exempt status. You can find a legal firm that will file the paperwork for you in exchange for a fee (usually a few hundred bucks), but I strongly recommend instead that you find an organization, like LCA, that will help you locate pro bono legal assistance from a law firm in your city or state. Such organizations include California Lawyers for the Arts (www .calawyersforthearts.org), Colorado Lawyers for the Arts (www.lawyersforthearts.org), Georgia Lawyers for the Arts (www.glarts.org), Seattle, Washington–based Washington Lawyers for the Arts (www.thewla.org), Washington, D.C.–based Washington Area Lawyers for the Arts (www.thewala .org), and New York City's Volunteer Lawyers for the Arts (www.vlany.org), just to name a few.

Incorporation and the Importance of Tax-Exempt Status

I can't reiterate enough how important it is to secure your tax-exempt status before you even begin to think about producing a show. It's much easier to raise money when people can use those donations as tax write-offs. Sure, you can gather nickels and dimes from your friends and family—but to get the big bucks you're going to need to launch your company, you simply must have that much-prized letter of tax exemption from the feds.

In order to file for tax-exempt status, you must first register your company with the Office of the Secretary of State (of the particular state you're headquartered in). You will file a document called "articles of incorporation," which serves as your company's "birth certificate." Its purpose is to inform your state government of the reason for your company's existence, as well as the names of the people who will be running it. Each state has its own articles of incorporation, and the form is available for download on most states' official Web sites.

Never lose sight of the fact that your small nonprofit theater company is, in reality, a serious corporation—a group of people who are legally authorized to act as an individual person and who are recognized by the law as a single entity.

TALK-BACK NOTES

- Establish a professional, diverse board of directors to guide the company and act as a liaison between the theater and its community.

- Don't be afraid to ask for a board fee when recruiting new members.

- Seek out guidance on incorporating, obtaining tax-exempt status, and other issues from qualified legal entities that offer their services to nonprofit companies on a pro bono basis.

5

CAPITAL

Investors, Grants, and
Your Company Budget

You need serious financing in order to launch your endeavor, and you cannot leave any stone unturned in your hunt for cash. Oftentimes artists have a tendency to downplay the importance of money, but if you don't have it, you won't even get your company off the ground, much less see it thrive. Therefore, you must worship your investors as ardently as the public worships movie stars and celebrity athletes. The secret is that *people invest in people*—so make sure that you handle the funds they bestow on you in a responsible manner and that you give your benefactors a good return on their investment.

When it comes to asking potential donors to part with some of their hard-earned cash to help fund your company, it's good practice to always ask for *more* than the amount you actually hope to receive. However, it also pays to be objective about your company's fundraising prospects. As the founder of a young company, you probably won't get far by running to the Ford Foundation and asking for a million dollars to launch your new theater. Be hopeful but also realistic when approaching potential funders. Most important, be sure that your passion, professionalism, and excitement about your new company shine through—inspiring potential benefactors to be equally excited. You must convey your excitement to your board of directors as well. Nothing helps you to raise money like having an energized board of directors who are eager to accomplish the challenge set in front of them.

Beginning Your Search for Funds

When it comes to locating potential sources of funds, perhaps the best place to begin is with your state's arts council. A major role of this organization is to fund local arts communities—and unlike many large corporations, state arts councils are generally willing to fund smaller start-up companies. In addition, your state arts council may act as a resource for finding other potential donors and identifying grants that you may qualify for at this early stage of the game.

Sponsorship

Before you can raise one red cent, you must put together a clever, well-written, and professionally proofread "sponsorship package"—a 10- to 12-page pamphlet that explains who you are, what you plan to do with the money you raise, and why what you plan to do is a valuable and noble endeavor that will provide countless rewards to your benefactors and their community. The package should contain the following.

- **Mission statement.** This should be the first thing a funder sees after turning the cover page.
- **History of the organization and its ensemble.** In this section, discuss your ensemble's background and training, identify the qualities that differentiate your ensemble from others in the area, share an inspiring story about how you selected the company's name, and explain why you chose this particular town, city, or neighborhood as your company's home.
- **Project description.** This section should include the titles of the plays you intend to produce in your inaugural season and a statement of your *dream* budget for the entire year. For example, your project description might be "$100,000 to cover the costs of all three of the season's productions as well as the operating expenses incurred in this season." The amount you state should be a somewhat inflated figure; you want to still be able to sustain the season even if you don't manage to raise the full amount.
- **Inaugural season rundown.** In this section, include a brief logline describing each play you intend to produce during your first season, and give the dates on which you intend to perform it. If you plan on producing a world premiere or Pulitzer Prize winner, now is the time to state that.
- **Target audience and anticipated impact.** Remember, you chose the location you did because you wanted to be near your target audience. In this section, explain what it is about your particular community that makes its members your target audience. Describe the impact you hope your works will have on the audience and the impact you hope to have on the community as a whole in years to come (if you

plan to someday offer acting classes or an educational outreach program for kids, this is the place to mention it).

- **Projected budget.** This is where you provide your (slightly inflated) budgeted projections in more detail. Include a breakdown of projected costs associated with the artistic staff, the production staff, marketing, public relations, education or community outreach programs, ticket services, postage, telemarketing, office supplies, insurance, and miscellaneous costs.

- **Sponsorship information.** Here you'll explain the different levels of sponsorship and the benefits associated with each level. For example, you might state that for a contribution of $10,000 or more, the donor becomes a member of the company's "founder's circle" and, as such, receives complimentary season tickets, an invitation to have dinner with the director, a free T-shirt, etc.

- **List of the members of your board of directors.** Include each board member's name, profession, and the position he or she holds on your company board (such as president or treasurer). Highlight the names of any major players who sit on your board, and consider including profiles on them to attract even more attention. Philanthropists in the community will be impressed to see that these respected people are involved with your company—so make sure their names jump off the page.

- **List of staff.** Include each staff member's name and position (artistic director, managing director, head of marketing, literary manager, director of arts in education, and so forth).

- **List of ensemble members.** Include the names and bios of each member of your ensemble. The bios of young actors probably won't include many stints at high-profile theaters, so play up each member's training and pedigree instead. (I don't care if an actor graduated from the Yale School of Drama or Pensacola Junior College; spin it in your favor.)

Remember, you are going to hand this out to the major players in your town. If you shortchange the sponsorship package, you shortchange the money. Short money equals short season!

The Budget

Before you can pitch a potential donor on funding your dream budget, you have to project what your real budget is going to be. As an example, the following is a breakdown of all the costs that a fictional theater company expects to incur during one season. I've broken it down into two budgets: the production budget, which covers all three of the company's planned productions for the season, and the operations budget, which covers all of the operating expenses for the same period. Rarely will funders want to see these figures itemized, but it's a great idea to have them (in slightly inflated form) just in case.

Below each budget is a list that describes each of that budget's line items. These lists are intended simply to provide you a more thorough idea of what's involved in each line item. They should not be included in the actual budgets you make available to potential funders.

LONG TAIL THEATRE COMPANY
Production and Operating Budgets

Seasonal Production Expenses

Actor Fees	$20,000
Director Fees	$15,000
Rent	$22,000
Lighting, Props, and Sound	$10,000
Advertising	$10,000
Stage Manager Fees	$6,000
Outside Service Fee	$4,000
Costumes	$3,000
Show Programs	$1,500
Photographs	$500
Total Production Expenses	**$92,000**

- **Actor Fees:** the total amount you plan to pay the actors for their work in the year's three productions (don't forget to include a cushion for understudies in that figure)
- **Director Fees:** the amount you plan pay the stage director or directors during the season
- **Rent:** the total cost of the space you lease to mount the season's productions; usually includes insurance costs
- **Lighting, Props, and Sound:** the total cost of the physical equipment and props you plan to purchase or rent in order to put on the season's productions
- **Advertising:** the total estimated cost of advertising (print ads, posters, postcards, etc.), as well as the marketing director's fee or stipend for the season
- **Stage Manager Fees:** includes both the stage manager's and the assistant stage manager's projected fees

- **Outside Service Fees:** any fees paid to costume, lighting, and set designers, photographers, and the like, who may not be a part of your ensemble
- **Costumes:** includes the cost of purchased materials or rented costumes
- **Show Programs:** the projected total cost of having the three shows' programs professionally produced and printed
- **Photographs:** the total cost of all expenses associated with the creation and printing of photographs to be distributed to the media during the season, including photographer fees

When Negotiating Fees, Start Low

Always try to negotiate fees that are less than the amount you've allotted in your budget. For example, if you've set aside $500 as an actor's fee for the run of a show, don't immediately offer him or her the full amount; start at $375 and barter from there.

Seasonal Operating Expenses

Office Expense	$3,000
Telephone/Answering Service	$2,000
Consultant Fees	$2,000
Postage and Delivery	$1,000
Web Site Maintenance	$1,000
Depreciation	$400
Licenses and Permits	$300
Bank Services	$200
Miscellaneous	$300
Total Operating Expenses	**$10,200**

- **Office Expense:** the total amount of rent that you will pay for office space this season (if your company's current office space is your apartment, list the total projected cost of company-related expenses for such items as paper, pens, printer cartridges, etc.)
- **Telephone/Answering Service:** the projected total cost for the season.
- **Consultants:** the total projected amount of any (very small) stipends that you might pay the artistic director or managing director, or any administrative fees you might incur, over the course of the season
- **Postage and Delivery:** the total projected cost of mailing promotional items and corresponding via conventional mail with various foundations, donors, and others during the season
- **Web Site Maintenance:** the projected (small) cost of having the company's Web site hosted and maintained for the season
- **Depreciation:** covers the wear and tear, and the associated loss of value, of the company's computer, fax machine, printer, etc. (this line item is strictly for tax purposes)
- **Licenses and Permits:** the total cost of obtaining or renewing licenses and permits during the season
- **Bank Services:** the total cost of doing business with the company's bank, including the printing of business checks
- **Miscellaneous:** covers unexpected small administrative expenses that you haven't budgeted for elsewhere but that inevitably pop up

Occasionally you might run across a potential benefactor who wants to see your line-item budget—but for the most part, the only figure you'll ever be asked about is the company's total budget for the season. In the case of our fictional company Long Tail, the total budget is *$102,200* ($92,000 for production expenses and $10,200 for operating expenses).

Leads

Many young actors believe that if they could just get in front of a few big-time stars and producers, they could secure the funds they need to launch their own theater company. Nothing could be further from the truth. In actuality, most "successful" (i.e., working) professionals are too damn busy trying to hold onto what little they have to turn around and help the little guy. With the exception of the *rare* few who've made millions of dollars and who now make it a point to give back to the arts, most professionals in the industry stick to working with people who are already working and to contributing to well-established programs. I know it sounds harsh, but that's just the way it is.

Believe it or not, when it comes to securing leads on potential benefactors, your biggest assets are your current or former classmates and good friends who are just starting out as well. It's best to start a conversation with your classmates *now*. Explain your plans of opening a theater company. You'll be surprised at who knows who and, more important, who's willing to help you.

Fresh out of graduate school, I was fortunate enough to be working at the Chicago Shakespeare Theatre along with a fellow classmate of mine named John Maclay. John told me about a "special friend" of his who was helping him found a Shakespeare company in Milwaukee. John knew I was opening a company of my own, and he wanted to introduce me to the man. After a week or so went by, I gathered our company's sponsorship package and headed north for Milwaukee. There, I met with this mysterious friend and, over breakfast, I spoke passionately about my vision for the new theater company. At the end of our conversation, I handed him the package and he handed me a check for $15,000. (Rest assured that I was only too happy to pick up the tab for breakfast.) Now, granted, most of this was luck—but what is luck, exactly? It's preparation meeting opportunity. When chance knocks, your bags have to be packed and you've got to be ready to go.

You can also find leads by attending plays produced by established theater companies and scouring the program for the list of benefactors. This is a very common practice, so don't feel that you're engaging in some sort of "arts espionage." If you attend the performance of a theater company that's similar to your own, chances are good that the same people who funded that company will take an interest in yours.

If you always present yourself in a serious, professional manner, you'll receive help. Never give up when it comes to raising money. I always held the belief that there was just too much money in our city for it not to come trickling down to us. If your mission is unique and original and you have the training to actually back up what you say, you may surprise some people and score some major, major, funds before you ever produce your first show.

Grants

Grant writing is a peculiar skill—but it's one that, with a little practice, can be mastered. Most local governments offer grant writing workshops to employees of nonprofit organization large and small. Here are some tips on grant writing from the Iowa Arts Council. These tips apply to most grants that involve the arts, regardless of where your company is located.

Getting Ready

1. Read the guidelines and be sure you understand them.
2. Be sure you're using current guidelines and the current application form.

Get the Basics

1. Did you provide the correct mailing address?
2. Have you entered the right Federal ID number?
3. Make sure e-mail addresses are correct and current.

Writing the Narrative

1. Answer all the narrative questions, and answer them in the order in which they're asked. Don't make reviewers search for the information they need.
2. Fresh, compelling approaches and ideas count. Redoing the same project you've produced for years make reviews think, "Been there, done that."
3. It's got to be about the arts. If reviewers have to search for the arts connection, it'll cost you points.
4. Assume the reviewers don't know you, your staff, your history, or what you do.
5. Read the review criteria and address them in your narrative. If they don't match what you want to do, maybe this isn't the right grant for you.
6. Back up your claims: If you say this is a "national model," that it's "never been done locally," and so forth, be sure to prove it.

7. Show direct, active methods of marketing and outreach that show you are truly reaching out to underserved or unserved audiences.

8. Take evaluation seriously, and show active methods of evaluating your work. Use forms, have focus groups, and assume that planning is part of evaluation. (What did you start out expecting? Where did you end up?)

The Budget and Support Materials

1. Use a calculator and make sure your figures are accurate and appropriate for the cost you're describing. Double check!

2. Excellent support materials will gain review points. Make sure you include relevant material in the proposal.

3. Support letters are not character references. If you include them, make sure they discuss your ability to make a success of the project you want.

4. Have someone proofread the application before you turn it in.

Stipends

Stipends are, basically, small payments made to people in the administration who are running the company, such as the marketing director, the managing director, and so forth. The purpose of a stipend is to compensate people for the time they put into the company, and stipends be really helpful in taking the financial strain off the ensemble. For example, at Congo Square, an ensemble member could get paid both an actor's fee for being in the production and an administrative stipend for performing the duties of marketing director. The amount of the stipend should be determined by the managing director in consultation with the artistic director. The costs associated with stipends should be part of the company's operations budget, not its production budget.

For the sake of transparency, never give one person the sole authority to sign stipend checks (or any other checks, for that matter). They should be cosigned either by the artistic director and the managing director or by the managing director and the board treasurer.

I suggest that you pay every administrative person the same amount when your company is just starting out. If, for example, your educational director is given a smaller stipend than your marketing director, it's likely that the educational director will begin to think that he or she isn't considered as important as the other guy. One person will certainly spend more time doing his or her job than the other will, but that's not really the point at this particular moment in the life of the organization. By paying every administrator the same amount, the company saves money and teamwork is encouraged.

That's something we *didn't* do at Congo Square, and it caused some arguments. The company was set up to incorporate, in some ways, a traditional theater hierarchy, with the artistic director and the managing director receiving more money than others in the company. This may not be the best way to set up a young organization. People can get extremely caught up in the meaning behind titles and compensation, and it can lead your company down a slippery slope.

As in any business, each member of the management team has to justify his or her paycheck. If ensemble members feel like the artistic director or the managing director isn't doing his or her job effectively, they have right to bring it up at a company meeting.

On a side note—I still believe that if the managing director and the artistic director are expected to do more for the company, then they should get paid more. The problem is that sometimes ensemble members do just as much if not more than the managing or artistic director. This is completely unacceptable, and it should be addressed immediately.

Sometimes a member of the staff also serves as a board member, in which case he or she will be in the awkward position of approving his or her own stipends. This can be a point of confusion and resentment by other members of the ensemble, who may misinterpret their colleague's compensation as payment for services rendered as a board member (which is illegal), and it may raise a red flag with the IRS as well. One way to avoid confusion is to draw up a contract for each position for which payment is made in exchange for labor. Those who serve in more than one paid position would receive a separate contract for each position.

An accurate and organized paper trail can save you many headaches and arguments—not just with the ensemble or the board of directors, but also with foundations and the omnipotent IRS.

A final note: Starting a theater company can be an extremely stressful and all-consuming endeavor for everyone concerned—so, *if* you can afford it, pay people for their labor. If you can only afford to pay them enough to cover the cost of a tank or two of gas, do that. Your colleagues will feel appreciated and things will run a lot more smoothly.

TALK-BACK NOTES

- When negotiating any fee or stipend, always offer less than the amount you've budgeted. This gives you room to negotiate—and it might allow you to save money that could be needed down the line.

- Be sure that your sponsorship package highlights or includes profiles of some of the more prominent board members of the organization. Their names lend an air of legitimacy to your new company that will go a long way in the philanthropic community.

- When searching for leads on people and organizations to approach for startup capital, don't overlook your friends and current or former classmates—they may have connections that can help you achieve your goals. In addition, attend the productions of theater companies that are similar to yours in size and focus, and search through their programs to see who funded them.

6

COMFORT

Rental Space, Safety, Transportation, and Food

Your theater company's first performance space should be discussed among all members of the organization, including both artistic and managing directors, the ensemble, and the board of directors. During the first season, everyone needs to take part in making the decision, to ensure that the needs of each member are considered and evaluated. Once a system for evaluating a space has been established, however, the decision of where to make a "home" should be left to the artistic director.

When thinking about your company's performance space, the word you need to keep in the back of your mind is *comfort*. The audience should feel comfortable making their way to the theater and relaxed once they're in it. Think of your theater company as being part of the hospitality business. Once you rent a theater from a landlord, you "own" it—it's now your home—so make the patrons feel as welcomed as you would guests in your own home. You can do this by offering small things like concessions and having some members of your ensemble who aren't performing in the production work the front of house and focus on building a great relationship with the community. Other details you need to focus on are safety concerns, availability of parking and/or public transportation, and proximity to restaurants, all of which impact your bottom line.

Your job as a founder is to consider and evaluate all of these particulars before you sign the deposit check for a performance space.

Nothing but the Rent

After you've secured your funds for the first season (or, at least, the first production), you and the posse are ready to hunt for an affordable performance space. In order to determine what "affordable" is, ask yourself, "How much can we *lose* on the space without going bankrupt after our first production?" In order to figure out what you can afford in rent, you need to estimate the number of tickets that will be sold (not given away, but *sold*) and determine the appropriate price for those tickets. In addition, you should make sure that your rent is no more than 25 percent of your total production budget.

Estimating Ticket Sales

Count on selling *half* the house for each performance. This is the basic rule for determining the rent you can afford and for evaluating whether or not the seating capacity of a space is going to meet your income needs. Never lose sight of the fact that you're going to be in a constant street fight for audience members. You're competing for their time and attention not only with other theater companies but also with the Internet, TV, films and DVDs, and video games, among other things. I don't mention this to discourage you but simply to persuade you to be realistic about the number of tickets you'll sell—and about the effort it's going to take to sell them. If you plan well and execute your strategy, I have no doubt you'll fly.

Setting the Ticket Price

Ticket prices should be high enough to allow you to bring in the income you need to pay the rent and other expenses, but low enough to be competitive with the theatrical productions of similarly sized companies. When setting ticket prices, also take into consideration the number of seats in the space and the total number of performances planned for the show. Congo Square's debut production, *The Piano Lesson*, was held in a 66-seat house and ran four nights a week. We set the ticket price for that show at $15. Had we sold out each performance—which we didn't—we would have made $3,960 per week. Fortunately, we knew to estimate that only half of the seats would be sold—and, I'm extremely pleased to say, we did accomplish that, clearing around $1,980 per week. After paying our weekly rent of $710, we were left with $1,270 to pay for other expenses.

Your rent for a particular show shouldn't be any more than a *quarter* of your total production budget for that show. If it's going to cost you $20,000 to produce a show, you want to spend no more than $5,000 on rent for the venue. Following this rule will help your new company avoid financial ruin if a show happens to bomb.

Safety

Physical Space

Safety issues concern not only patrons who attend but also the actors performing in the space. Many urban areas have plenty of storefront theaters the size of someone's living room. Although these can offer an exhilarating experience, they might also be firetraps—many of them do not meet city fire codes. Keep this little detail in mind when you're looking at possible venues and some slumlord is offering you a major deal on rent. Don't saddle yourself with a place that could be shut down by city inspectors at any moment—and that puts your patrons in physical danger.

Neighborhood

Who patronizes the theater more than anyone else? *Women!* If the group that makes up the majority of the audience does not feel safe in the neighborhood in which your performance space is located, your actors will be performing to an empty house. Sure, you can negotiate a sweet deal with a landlord for cheap rent and the use of that large parking lot next door, but if the space is near some housing projects (and I can say this because *I'm* from the projects), people won't come. It doesn't matter that the neighborhood is changing; it doesn't matter that there are many honest, hardworking people living in that community. In our business, perception is everything. If people are going to give you their hard-earned money, they are going to want to feel safe while they're making their way to your location and watching your show—and they have every right to want that.

Make sure the theater space you rent is at least located on a well-lit street, and always keeping in mind the security of your patrons (especially your female patrons). Before you rent a space, drive through the area late at night and talk with someone at a nearby police station or with a neighborhood watch group to gauge how safe the area is.

Box Office

Some theaters that rent space also offer box office personnel to assist in taking ticket orders. This service usually costs a hell of a lot of money, but sometimes it can be tempting to go for it. Box office and other front-of-the-house duties are a straight-up pain, especially for actors who would much rather be on stage instead of dealing with patrons' complaints. Well, welcome to the wonderful world of show business. You had better grow a thick skin, roll up your sleeves, and get dirty handling your own box office, because if this important duty isn't taken care of in an efficient and cost-effective way, your company could close after one performance.

Why do I recommend renting out a theater that allows *you*, not your landlord, to run your box office? One—it will be cheaper. Two—you need the experience. And three—your patrons need to be introduced not only to the actors in the production but also to the people behind the scenes who are responsible for making the magic happen. Actors and audiences alike can easily forget that theater is a team sport and that the ensemble includes the administrative staff as well as the artists. When an actor in your company is not cast in a show, he or she should be working behind the scenes to get the current production mounted.

As is the case with most new ensemble companies, Congo Square's actors *were* its administrative staff in the early years. For our first production, *The Piano Lesson*, I ran the box office and managed the other front-of-the-house duties. This included taking cash from patrons at the door, working with volunteer usher staff, cleaning the lobby, tending to our landlord's requests or concerns, and depositing the money in the bank at the end of each week. It was a thankless job, but if I wanted to make sure that the company enjoyed a successful launch, it was also a vital one.

Parking and Transportation

When scouting a space, consider whether or not there will be sufficient parking or public transportation available. This could make or break you. I don't care if it's friends, family, coworkers, associates, spouses, girlfriends, boyfriends, whatever—if it's a hassle to get to or park at your theater, that's a wrap; game over. I'm not suggesting that you need to find a space that offers valet parking—but you do need to make sure that your venue is in close proximity to an affordable parking lot and a subway station or frequently serviced bus stop.

Here are a few things to keep in mind when it comes to parking and transportation.

- The areas between the theater and the parking lot, subway station, and bus stop should be well lit and worry free in terms of safety.
- Public transportation that services the area should run well into the night on both weekdays and weekends. Review the train and bus schedules.

- If you are counting on ample street parking, make several trips to the area at the hour you anticipate patrons will need to arrive for the show. In some areas, finding a place to park on the street may be easy during the day but impossible at night. Also, make sure that during the hours that your theater will be hosting patrons, street parking is not limited to those with permits.
- If your patrons will need to park in commercial parking lots or garages, make sure they offer affordable hourly rates. See if you can negotiate a deal that allows your patrons to park at a discounted rate.
- Be sure that your Web site features a map of the area, directions to the theater, and information on parking and public transportation options.

For our first show, patrons had a hard time finding parking near the theater because of construction that was going on in the area. Fortunately, the venue was located right next to a subway station, and we made sure to highlight that on our Web site and in our postcards. I'm positive that our proximity to public transportation saved us from what could have been a disastrous outcome.

Food

If you can find theater space near a good restaurant, that can be a tremendous bonus. Most people like to make a night out at the theater an event, and that includes both dinner and a show. Do some research to pinpoint the hottest restaurants in your area. Oftentimes, some of the best chefs in town own low-key venues that are "hidden in plain sight" and that cater to a very sophisticated clientele. If you find a venue near one of these establishments, develop a good relationship with the manager and offer to promote the restaurant in your programs if, say, the restaurant displays posters or postcards that promote whatever show you're putting on at the moment. In fact, you should cultivate relationships with the owners and managers of *all* of the restaurants in your area. This is particularly true of restaurants that have only recently opened. The only thing tougher than opening a new theater company is opening a new restaurant. Both establishments are going to need a steady flow of patrons in order to survive—so why not band together to do some cross-promotion?

Regardless of the number of restaurants in your area, consider offering food and beverages at the theater itself via a concessions stand. People love to grab a drink and nibble on peanuts, ice cream, etc. during a show's intermission, and your company can earn some extra income by offering these items for purchase. In addition, you can use the concessions stand as an opportunity to socialize and connect with your patrons. If possible, negotiate a rental agreement that allows you to install and run your own concessions area. (Some theater owners insist on selling their own products in the lobby.)

TALK-BACK NOTES

- Your rent for a particular show should be no more than 25 percent of the production budget for that show.

- When selecting a venue, remember that patrons and ensemble members must feel safe in both the theater and its neighborhood, and make sure that parking and public transportation are readily accessible.

- At least for the first season, have someone in your company run the box office and handle other front-of-the-house duties. This helps to build good relations with patrons and goes a long way toward ensuring that your inaugural season is a success.

- Food and theater go hand in hand. Cultivate good relationships and pursue cross-promotional opportunities with the restaurants near your venue, and consider installing a concessions stand in the theater lobby.

7

TEAMWORK

Artistic and
Administrative Positions

No man is an island, and a theater company proves that point. It is a very tight unit—so tight that if one person screws up, it could cost you the game. This chapter details exactly the kind of commitment you're going to need and expect out of your ensemble.

The most important job positions for a young theater company to fill are on the artistic staff: those of the artistic director, production manager, director of arts in education, and literary manager. The administrative staff, which includes the managing director and the marketing director, work with the artistic director to figure out the best way to promote the mission of the company. Research these positions using the outlines later in the chapter, and determine which ensemble member is the best fit for each one. For example, if someone in the ensemble is particularly friendly, outgoing, and great with young people, you may want to assign him or her the job of director of arts in education, to harness that energy for your community outreach program.

A theater company is only as strong as the weakest link in its chain of command. I know it sounds cliched, but as the late Mike Malone (a professor of mine at Howard University) once told me, "Cliches work; that's why they're cliches."

Every member of a start-up theater company is taking on enormous responsibility, and you need to take the time to write out the job descriptions of each position so that everyone can see what lies ahead and what is expected of each member of the company. I strongly believe the ensemble should be well aware of the duties and responsibilities of the two leaders—the artistic and managing directors—as well. If all members are aware of one another's job, they feel like they're in the loop, and everyone can stay in his or her respective lane.

It will surely take some time—maybe a year or two—to figure out which ensemble member is best suited to which position. Early on, people might choose jobs that may not be right for them. Circumstances might change, too. For example, someone who decides to become a parent might not be able or willing to commit as much time to the company as he or she used to. Life happens, so be prepared to roll with it.

Double-Time

As the founder of a theater company, you must make sure the ensemble realizes that they will work double duty for the first couple of years. Everyone must understand that no one has the luxury of participating only when he or she is cast in a show.

All ensemble members have to take on multiple roles: actor/ marketing director; actor/artistic director; actor/managing director; and so on. This sounds obvious, but believe me, you will be surprised by the number of people who say they want to form a theater company, then refuse to get their hands dirty (literally) by striking a set.

The problem is that you do not know what kind of soldiers you have until you are in the heat of battle. Here's a piece of personal advice: if you have a talented actor in your ensemble who does not want to do any kind administrative or production work, *get rid of him or her.* That person will be toxic to the group as a whole, and you're better off without people like that. An individual's acting talent can only serve your organization so much. In the beginning, you need discipline, talent, and teamwork in order to get the job done.

Think about it: if a quarter of the ensemble wants only to act and will not commit to doing the behind-the-scenes work of production or administration, you will not have a company. An ensemble member with any form of laziness must be weeded out and uprooted at the outset.

Positions

Now that the ensemble realizes that more than acting is needed to launch the company, it is time to put your aces in their proper places. You and the rest of the group have to figure out what each member is good at or passionate about *other than* acting. Plenty of jobs need to be taken care of before lift-off. Ideally, ensemble members will participate in deciding who does what, and in choosing the job at which they believe they will excel.

When I founded Congo Square, I quickly took the job of managing director, while Derrick Sanders assumed the role of artistic director. We ran the company like a football team: Derrick was in charge of the artistic staff, (the "offense") while I looked over the administrative staff (the "defense"). We made sure all members were suited for the positions they chose or were assigned, and the ensemble made sure we played our roles as artistic and managing directors properly. By dividing the responsibilities, Derrick and I found the company easier to manage, and we were able to get things done smoothly and efficiently.

Here are the six essential positions that you must fill in order to launch your company, along with a rundown of each position's responsibilities.

Artistic Staff

Artistic oversight of the theater company and its programs is the duty of the *artistic director*. The person in this position is also responsible for assuring that the company fulfills its contractual obligations and maintains productive working relationships with its constituents. The artistic director recognizes the managing director as an equal, and he or she serves as a community liaison for the company.

The artistic director can report directly to either the board of directors or the ensemble, depending on how you want the company structured. I would recommend that the ensemble members evaluate the artistic director's performance—after all, they're the artists and they are the ones who work with him or her every day. Also, the ensemble is better qualified to evaluate the success or failure of a production from an artistic standpoint.

The artistic director's responsibilities are as follows.

- Promote the long-term well-being of the company while maintaining the integrity of the mission statement at all times
- Review productions for artistic quality and financial efficiency
- Create and present assessments of the ensemble and recommendations regarding it to the board of directors
- Supervise the theater's artistic departments
- In collaboration with the managing director, formulate and negotiate all contracts for goods and services provided to the theater
- In collaboration with the managing director, participate in the organization of all fundraising events
- Attend all fundraising events
- In collaboration with the managing director, make all decisions regarding hiring, firing, and disciplinary action
- Oversee the development of the company's education and outreach programs
- In collaboration with the managing director, formulate and establish long-term company goals
- Perform or oversee other duties as required by the ensemble

The *production manager* oversees all the production departments of the company and implements creative solutions that most effectively realize productions within time, budgetary, and space constraints. He or she reports only to the artistic director.

Because it requires very specific skill sets, the position of production manager should not be filled by an actor but instead by a qualified lighting and set designer—or, ideally, by a technical director.

The production manager's responsibilities are as follows.

- Supervise and facilitate the production process, including planning and scheduling, budgeting and allocating resources, contracting employees and designers, facilitating preproduction design meetings, and monitoring progress of all production elements
- Negotiate individual contracts for designers, composers, and coaches
- Approve all hirings and terminations and monitor employee performances
- Develop and maintain annual production budgets for the following areas: all designers, stage management, scenery, props, paint, and running crew; authorize expenditures within set limits in these areas
- Track and control expenditures to ensure that all projects come in under budget
- Anticipate budget problems and alert the artistic director of any potential cost overruns
- Perform other duties as assigned by the artistic director

The *director of arts in education* is responsible for creating and maintaining an artistic relationship between your company and local schools by developing and implementing programs designed to broaden students' exposure to theater and to familiarize them with your company's own aesthetic. He or she reports only to the artistic director.

The director of arts in education's responsibilities are as follows.

- Create and allocate the budget for the company's education department
- Oversee all education and community outreach programs, which may include classes, training programs, and educational touring shows
- Maintain schedules, calendars, correspondence, and communications with schools, parents, and teachers
- Coordinate teacher seminars, student matinee performances, school visits, parent programs, post-performance discussions, and backstage tours
- Oversee the writing of and edit all teacher and student study guides
- Research and write grants
- Maintain and allocate the fiscal budget set by artistic director
- Create annual final reports and submit them to corporate, foundation, and government donors
- Perform other duties as assigned by artistic director

The *literary manager* is responsible for handling, overseeing, or assisting with virtually every task involved in the selection of plays that are to be produced by the company. He or she reports only to the artistic director.

The literary manager's responsibilities are as follows.

- Read all plays that are being considered for production; create and present detailed synopses of each play to the ensemble
- Assist the artistic director in obtaining rights to produce plays and in finding plays that are requested by the ensemble
- Photocopy and file scripts for use by the ensemble; ensure access to scripts on file
- Maintain company archives

- Create, schedule, and lead a program of playwriting workshops
- Serve as or secure the services of a dramaturge as needed
- Perform other duties as assigned by the artistic director

Administrative Staff

The *managing director* is responsible for the administrative oversight of the theater company and its programs. He or she is responsible for ensuring that the company fulfills its contractual obligations and that it maintains productive working relationships with its constituents. As such, he or she also serves as a community liaison for the company. The managing director reports directly to the board of directors and recognizes the artistic director as an equal.

The managing director's responsibilities are as follows.

- Promote the long-term well-being of the company while maintaining the integrity of the company's mission statement at all times
- Create and maintain financial reports and budgets and submit them to the board of directors.
- Formulate the company's administrative policies and procedures, including those that pertain to personnel.
- Review quality and financial effectiveness of all productions and report assessments and recommendations to program directors and the board of directors
- Supervise the company's administrative departments and work with them to formulate their development plans
- Head all fundraising initiatives

- In collaboration with the artistic director, make all decisions regarding hiring, firing, and disciplinary action
- Review and approve all salary requests and adjustments
- Review all contracts for goods and services provided to the theater
- Function as the final fiscal authority on all corporate disbursements: review and approve all requests for payments and sign all corporate checks, including payroll checks, according to policies and procedures established by the board of directors
- Perform other duties as may be assigned by the board of directors

The *marketing director* is responsible for all aspects of marketing, distribution, and communications to the general public and media. He or she reports to the managing director.

The responsibilities of the marketing director are as follows.

- Oversee and manage group sales, telemarketing, and individual ticket subscriptions
- Oversee and manage advertising and public relations endeavors
- Implement and evaluate strategic business and marketing plans, such as coproductions with other theater companies or partnerships with other nonprofit organizations
- Create well-researched and well-analyzed revenue forecasts
- Develop and gain approval of strategic plans for all projects and tasks to reach revenue goals

- Write an annual plan based on research and a careful analysis of lessons learned as a result of the past year's efforts
- Develop plans to raise awareness of the theater company among potential theater patrons
- Create all advertisements, press releases, newsletters, brochures, and playbills
- Manage all fiscal planning endeavors (e.g., expense reports or sales projection reports) and analyze marketing and box office for effectiveness and profit

Components of a Solid Strategic Plan

A carefully crafted strategic plan for meeting revenue goals includes measurable objectives, explanations of how those objectives will be achieved, descriptions of the tasks involved (and the proposed dollar amount to be budgeted for each task), and time lines for accomplishing the tasks and objectives. Strategic plans should also include a competitive analysis and thoughtful discussions regarding product, pricing, sales, advertising and public relations, and promotions.

These positions may sound like a lot of work—and they are!—but with the exception of the production manager position, all of the roles listed can be performed by actors.

As long as the managing director and the artistic director are constantly communicating with each another, the speed bumps should be minimal. These days, thanks to iPhones, BlackBerries, etc., there is no excuse for the left hand not knowing what the right hand is doing, and team members should be able to get in touch with one another at a moment's notice whenever a decision must be made or a problem or opportunity arises.

As the ensemble members commit to either the artistic ("offensive") or administrative ("defensive") positions of *their* choice, they will need to do extensive reading, research, and flexing of some serious business-skill muscles they may not be used to using. Reassure them—and yourself—that they can, indeed, handle their responsibilities. We did it at Congo Square, and you can do it, too. Of course, in order for them to succeed, the members of your ensemble must have the *desire* to succeed—both individually and as a team

A final thought regarding positions: In football and in the running of a theater company, the offense gets all the glory—but it's the defense that wins the game. You might find the administrative ("defensive") positions a tough sell compared to those on the artistic ("offensive") side of the fence. Make sure everyone understands how vital *every* role—administrative as well as artistic—is to the company.

TALK-BACK NOTES

- Theater is very much a team sport, so it is imperative that you found your organization with team players, not with glory hounds. Your company will fail if you populate it with people who simply want to act and do nothing else.

- Ask your actors what other jobs they'd like to perform, and have each one work on that position's job description with you. This way, they'll be more involved in the building process and more likely to hold themselves accountable for their duties behind the scenes.

8

BUZZ

Publicity and Marketing

In this 21st-century world of the Internet, a million cable and public access channels, and countless magazines and newspapers, you must become a master of the spin. The problem for today's media is that there are far too many distribution outlets and not enough content for them to program. As long as your work is exceptional and commands attention, you should find that local media is more than happy to report on your company and its productions. The problem for *you* is to create that media and community hype without looking desperate. It should be the goal of everyone in the organization—board, ensemble, artistic director, etc.—to gain positive exposure for the new company in any way they can, without sacrificing their confidence, professionalism, or passion.

Generating Hype

Before anyone can purchase a ticket to attend your opening production, he or she must first know about your company. As they say in Hollywood, "It doesn't matter who you know; it matters who knows you." The same can be said for the theater. You'll have an easier time introducing your theater to its community if people have already been made aware of your company via media coverage and public buzz.

Before starting your publicity push, you must be in a position to capitalize on the growing hype. Make sure your logo has been designed, your business cards have been printed and are ready to be handed out, and your Web site has been designed and loaded with information and is up and running (see the next section). While the marketing director is responsible for ensuring that all of these tasks are completed, he or she can't execute them alone. The help of both the artistic and the managing director, if not the entire ensemble, will be required.

Once you've secured the participation of respectable mentors and advisors who have agreed to lend their names and legitimacy to the company, your next order of business is to start generating that media hype. Send out a brief press release to local media that announces the founding of the company and offers some key points on who's involved and what your first season will look like. In Congo Square's initial press release, we announced to the Chicago media that we were a new company, that we were based on the West Side, and that our advisory board members included such luminaries as actor Harry Lennix, playwright August Wilson, director Chuck Smith, and actor Al Freeman Jr. As a result, our company received some much-appreciated initial press coverage. A major local newspaper printed a blurb about Congo Square in its Arts section, listing the productions of our upcoming season as well as an office telephone number that people could call for more information. (It was actually my home phone number; in those days, my apartment *was* our office.) People saw the blurb, and they actually started calling to get tickets a full two months before we launched our first production.

Of course, it's not enough for the media to hype your company; you also have to get the public talking about it. To generate buzz at the grass-roots level, consider creating and both giving away and selling T-shirts that feature your logo and Web address—and, I suggest, an intriguing quote to capture people's attention. (A quote we had on one of our shirts was "If you want drama . . . turn off the TV!" It may sound corny now, but it was extremely effective.) This can create great word of mouth as people begin to see the T-shirts all over town.

For the T-shirts you give away for free, the most cost-effective strategy is to give them to the people who are likely to generate the maximum amount of buzz for your company by wearing them. For example, you may want to focus on getting your T-shirt into the hands (and on the backs) of prominent members of the community who come into contact with a large and diverse section of the local population, such as restaurant managers, personal trainers, and corporate professionals. Make sure you've established a rapport with the person you're giving your T-shirt to; that dramatically increases the chances that he or she will actually wear it around town—and talk up your theater to anyone who asks about it—instead of just throwing the shirt in a drawer.

Your Web Site and the Internet

Thanks to technology, there are numerous ways to connect with potential patrons, funders, and the all-important media.

In this day and age, your company's Web site is as important as its name and mission statement. It's your face to the outside world. Patrons expect professional companies to have professional-looking Web sites, and yours will serve as an advertisement and marketing tool for your business 24 hours a day, seven days a week. If you don't have any idea how your site should look or what it should contain, simply visit other theater companies' sites for inspiration. Now, you won't be able to afford the flashy designs featured on the Web sites of the Public or the Old Globe, but you will come away with ideas about content. If you can't afford a full Web site initially, set up a MySpace or Facebook page for your company until you get on your feet.

A great Web designer can be worth his or her weight in gold, so take the time to search one out. Pay only what you can afford, but make sure that the site looks like a million bucks and inspires people to give money. I don't care if you don't know the dates of your first production or even what the production will be—have a designer put *something* up on your site. Showcase the ensemble by featuring their headshots and biographies; list the advisors and board members; and explain the name of the new company and how it came about. Remember to include your contact information as well.

Be sure to feature the Web site URL on the company's business cards; as everyone in your organization begins to network and pass out the cards, the URL will drive traffic to the site. Many times you may not be able to give someone you've just met the full pitch of the company, so you're going to have to refer them to the Web site. Upon reviewing that site, he or she should leave excited and ready to write you a check.

The wonderful thing about the Internet is that it makes information on your company available to a global audience. During our first production of *The Piano Lesson*, we were shocked to a see a tall, elegant German couple in the audience. After the show, we asked them how they'd heard about us, and they said they'd seen our Web site when they were looking for things to do in Chicago.

Look into advertising your company and its productions on others' Web sites as well as on your own. Newspapers are currently dying a slow, painful death. Instead of spending your resources on a print ad, it is better to advertise your show online. If you want to advertise in the *Village Voice* or the *Washington Post*, go for an ad that appears on the publication's Web site instead of one that appears in the print version of its publication. You'll reach a million times the number of people online as you would in print, and who knows—you just may get an elegant couple from Germany at one of your productions.

Blogs and Podcasts

Recent years have seen the rise of two additional opportunities for Internet marketing: blogs and podcasts. Blogs are personal journals that people post online, detailing their thought and ideas on countless topics both profound and mundane, from global hunger to sports to cooking. Starting an official blog on your theater company's Web site is the perfect way to share the behind-the-scenes details of its growth and development with interested readers all over the world. Anyone in your organization can contribute, and by doing so they build online relationships that can very easily translate into audience members for your upcoming productions.

Podcasts are audio files that you record and upload to your Web site for people to download to their computer, phone, or iPod. They are another excellent way to cultivate a relationship with current and potential audience members. For example, you could find an affordable recording studio and record your ensemble reading a few scenes from plays the company is considering producing. Upload them to your Web site and have your fans vote on which play they want to see your troupe perform. By interacting with your audience early and often, and encouraging them to contribute personally to your company's development, you almost guarantee that more of them will show up for your performances.

The Internet has also changed how companies handle press releases. Only eight or nine years ago, one had to fax a release and physically deliver accompanying photos to publications editors. Today, newspapers and other publications prefer that you e-mail both press releases and photos. The standard procedure is to send out each press release twice—first a month in advance of the event you are announcing, and again a week before the event (or, in the case of a play, its first preview). You must put everything in the release that you feel a newspaper critic or an editor would take an interest in or would be willing to cover in a story. The press release should include the following in a clear and concise manner.

- Name of theater company
- Play and playwright
- Director and cast
- Synopsis
- Dates and show times
- Ticket price
- Box office number and company Web site address
- Venue
- Company history

Here's a copy of our very first press release for *The Piano Lesson*.

FOR IMMEDIATE RELEASE

DATE

**CONGO SQUARE THEATRE COMPANY
PRESENTS**
AUGUST WILSON'S
THE PIANO LESSON
Directed by Ron OJ Parson

This exuberant drama deals with a family's haunting legacy. Congo Square Theatre Company is proud to present, in its inaugural season, the 10th-anniversary production of this Pulitzer Prize–winning play from one of America's greatest playwrights.

Featuring: Aaron Todd Douglas, Libya Pugh, Derrick Sanders, Will Sims II, Ann Joseph, Charles Michael Moore, J. J. McCormick, Amber Dorbin, and Lanisha Yates.

October 19–November 18, 2000
Thursday–Saturday: 7:30 P.M.
Sunday: 3:00 P.M.

CHICAGO DRAMATISTS THEATRE
1105 W. Chicago Avenue

Tickets: $15

For reservations, call: 773-###-####
For more information, visit: www.congosquaretheatre.org

ABOUT CONGO SQUARE: Congo Square Theatre Company is an ensemble dedicated to artistic excellence. In producing definitive and transformative theater spawned from the African diaspora, as well as other world cultures, Congo Square Theatre Company seeks to establish itself as an institution of multicultural theater.

"Friendraisers"

A month or so before your first production, host a "friend-raiser." The focus of this event shouldn't be on raising funds but on raising *awareness*. Invite the potential patrons who've seen press about you and expressed interest in coming to see your productions, people who have already donated, college alumni, old high school buddies, other actors and artists, local entrepreneurs, community leaders (such as your community alderman or councilman), and, of course, the board members. In fact, the board of directors should host the function, and each member should invite his or her own personal contacts to the event. (Congo Square was fortunate enough to have a great board of directors from the very beginning. Les Coney, Roxanne Ward, Luis Lewin, and Lester Detterbeck were all instrumental in making sure the company got off on the right foot.)

Many new board members can be recruited as a result of small, intimate functions such as friendraisers. Most corporate people love to socialize, and live theater is a great venue for them to do so. Make sure that during the event, you have a sign-in sheet for guests so that you can reach out to them once your first production opens. The sign-in sheet should include spaces for a guest's name, telephone number, and e-mail address. This will probably be your first social event in the community, so don't be shy—it's your opportunity to sell the company to people who have already demonstrated genuine enthusiasm and passion for theater and for your endeavor. It's also a good idea to have a photographer present to capture the function so that you can post photos of the event and the people who attended it to your Web site. And don't forget to invite the local press to cover your event!

The artistic director can organize scenes for the ensemble to showcase at the friendrasier, or you can choose not to showcase the ensemble at that time and instead simply invite people to come party. Your job as the founder is to make sure that guests are having a good time and that they are socializing with the actors in the ensemble as well as with one another. Once people get to know the members of your group on a personal level, they will feel more obligated to come out and support them. If people have a great time, they'll go back to work the next day talking about your new company and how excited they are to see your first show. Positive word of mouth such as this is invaluable; you should never underestimate its power.

TALK-BACK NOTES

- Once you have secured your advisory board and your board of directors, distribute a brief press release that explains who you are, where you're located, who's involved (such as well-known members of your boards), and what plays you're planning to produce during your first season. About a month before each production, distribute a press release giving the details of the play and how to get tickets for it. About a week before you preview each play, send that press release out again.

- Your Web site should be well thought out and designed. Remember that it is, essentially, an online commercial that promotes your new theater company to the world 24/7.

- The purpose of holding a "friendraiser" is to recruit more board members and to introduce, in the friendly context of a social gathering, your ensemble to potential patrons and others who've expressed interest in your work. Invite everyone you know—including the media.

9

COMMUNITY

Education, Outreach,
and Discount Programs

I t's not enough for you to simply enrich your audiences' lives through your performances; if you want more from your community, you have to *give* more—through education and outreach initiatives and discount programs. The most difficult thing about running a nonprofit business is that you must find the appropriate balance between art and commerce. You must fulfill not only your obligation to yourselves and your audiences by performing cutting-edge, enlightening pieces of work but also your obligations to your community at large by providing valuable enrichment to its people—all while running the company as the business it truly is, always keeping an eye on the bottom line. Theaters have been struggling to perform all of these duties simultaneously since before you were born, and they will continue to do so long after you're gone.

However, I still believe that a theater can "have its cake" by producing great art and "eat it too" by making sure that

101

art is profitable and that the company is of value to its artists, audiences, and community alike. It sometimes helps to think about your company in the grander scheme of the cultural landscape. We're constantly giving of ourselves, both our time and our effort. By focusing some of that time and effort on the community at large, you'll be weaving your theater into the very fabric of that community—and that can only mean more patrons for your business.

Education and Outreach

Let's face it—if the theater is going to survive well into the 21st century, it's going to have to cultivate young audiences. Technology is making it more and more convenient for young people to entertain themselves at home. What with video games and the Internet, kids aren't as active as they used to be, which is resulting in all kinds of problems, from childhood obesity to teens feeling alienated from the world around them—and that's where your company's education and outreach endeavors can step in to help not only the community but society as a whole.

In order for an outreach program to work, you're going to need at least 10 people actively participating in it. While some ensemble members are gearing up for your first production, others in your company should be working with the arts-in-education director, in collaboration with a local community center, to assist area kids via a strong arts program of activities, such as helping children to put on their own production.

I'm proud to say that before we had a dime, our ensemble was deep in the trenches on the West Side of Chicago working with the James Jordan Club, a chapter of the Boys and Girls Clubs of Chicago. Javon Johnson, Congo Square's literary manager and a playwright, wrote an original play for the kids, which they rehearsed over several weeks before performing in front of their parents and staff. Our work there helped to introduce us to the community, and it gave the club an opportunity to offer an arts program in addition to its usual sports-oriented curriculum. Some of the kids we worked with even went on to star in our first production, which exposed them to professional theater. I know this sounds like a lot of work, and it is! But Congo Square did it, and so can you. The ensemble may be skeptical and feel overwhelmed initially, but you must inspire and motivate them to follow through. Trust me, few people are excited about the prospect of working with challenging kids, but the satisfaction of watching those kids perform can oftentimes be worth the agony.

Of course, it's best to match each member of your ensemble with the nonperforming roles for which he or she is best suited, so if someone in your ensemble truly isn't good with children, don't involve that person in endeavors that deal with kids. But remember that no one in the company has the luxury of simply acting; in order for the company to even survive, much less thrive, each must perform other duties as well. It's simply a matter of letting each one pick his or her "poison."

Keep in mind, too, that working with the community can be very time consuming and stressful—if you don't soon figure out a way to pay ensemble members for their outreach work, you will lose people left and right. Young actors usually have no problem *performing* for no pay, but you can't expect them to work in the hood for nothing forever. After you secure your tax exempt status (which will allow you to raise more money), the actors working on outreach programs should be the *first* ensemble members paid for their services.

Another important reason to begin work on a program of community education and outreach as soon as possible is that proof of such efforts help to expedite your 501(c)(3) status, and your work will give you something to talk up in your grant applications. It's also good for everyone to keep in mind that most of the members of your ensemble will eventually earn a living from the company through its arts-in-education program. As a professional actor, you aren't always guaranteed a job—but if, in between acting gigs, you can rely on steady, paying work in your own company's well-funded children's program, you're leaps and bounds ahead of your peers in terms of financial security.

Discounts

Let me be the first to say that I *hate* giving discounts. People are always trying to get something for nothing, and as a producer, you want them to pay for the entertainment and enrichment you provide. This is a business, and your company can't grow if it constantly gives away its merchandise. However, at this stage of the game—the launch of your first season—it's more important to get butts in the seats than it is to make money at the box office. Just be smart about whom you hand out your free tickets to. Just as you want to focus on giving away promotional T-shirts to key influential people, you want to make sure your free tickets get into the hands of those who will promote your company to the general public—local bartenders, restaurant managers, barbershop and beauty salon owners, and so forth. Think of your ticket giveaways as a short-term investment in the success of your company, and do your best to make sure that investment pays off.

You want your theater packed for each performance night after night, so hopefully you've chosen a small theater in a good neighborhood and offered reasonable ticket prices. If the theater isn't at least half full during the run of your first production, it could prove disastrous for the company in terms of morale. Everyone in the ensemble and in the organization as a whole needs to feel that their hard work is paying off, so you have do everything humanly possible to make sure that people come to your first production. Here are several discount options and the reasons why you should—or should not—consider them.

Tickets to *previews* should be sold as "two for the price of one." Since the play is technically still in rehearsal and is therefore not a finished product, give the early birds a break on the ticket price. Also, because these people have gotten a discount, they will be more likely to recommend the production to other people, thus building word of mouth for the main run.

Slow nights are also a good time to consider discount pricing. Thursday was always a notoriously slow night for theaters both big and small in Chicago, so Congo Square offered "two for one Thursdays." If you know ahead of time that it's likely you'll be playing to an empty house on any particular day, it's best to offer some kind of discount on the price of that day's tickets. You want the actors performing at their best, and that usually requires having patrons in the seats to play to. In addition, you don't want a potential donor to arrive on a slow night and find only 10 audience members in the house and a cast that, as a result, seems off its game.

Ticket sales to *groups* of 10 or more people are often discounted. I would offer a 15 percent discount to groups during at least your first year; during that crucial initial season, it's more important that people see your production and performers than it is to make money. If enough people fall in love with your work, the money will follow. Keep in mind, however, that a group of 30 can become a much smaller group of 15 in a New

York minute; for that reason, group purchases should always be paid in advance, on a nonrefundable basis.

Senior citizens and students are two demographic groups to which I would suggest *not* extending a special discount (at least during your first year), mainly because there's really nothing stopping a person in either of these categories from taking advantage of other discounts you offer. If your ticket prices are reasonable (and they'd better be, since you're new on the scene), there's no reason that senior citizens and students shouldn't be able to pay for one. When you have your own space and a permanent administrative staff, then you can include senior and student discounts. Until then, direct them to take advantage of the discounts offered for previews and slow nights.

TALK-BACK NOTES

- Before you even launch your first production, work with a community center to produce an education and outreach program. This is a perfect way to introduce your new company to the community, and your arts-in-education endeavors will both help you to secure your tax exempt status and allow you to qualify for additional grants.

- In order for your company to survive, every member of your ensemble must willingly take on a variety of responsibilities and tasks, including participating in community education and outreach endeavors. But try to match each actor to the role that best suits him or her, and make sure that participants in your outreach programs are the *first* ensemble members who are paid for their services when funds become available.

- During your first year, count on giving away a significant number of tickets and offering discounts in order to fill seats. Focus on giving tickets to those who are likely to talk up your company to others, and be selective about what types of discounts to offer.

10

FEEDBACK

Previews, Critics, and Audience Assessments

Your power as a theater will always reside with people—not just those within your organization but also those in your community. The reason why the large LORT (League of Resident Theatres) Equity theaters receive huge corporate funding while small or midsized organizations that *actually* need it are left to struggle with smaller donations is that only the large houses can guarantee that large audiences will see that corporation's logo in the program or on a poster in the lobby. Corporations are usually more interested in advertising than they are in philanthropy. Nevertheless, even without the benefit of six- or seven-figure donations, as long as you listen to what the people of your community want and you find a way to fulfill those desires while staying true to your company's aesthetic, you'll win in the long run. This chapter explores the various ways in which you can solicit, obtain, and use feedback from your ensemble, the critics, and your audiences.

Previews

I would suggest that you offer as many previews you can afford to put on. If you rent a space for six weeks, the first two of those weeks should be devoted to previews. This does two things: first, it creates goodwill (and good word of mouth) in the community because locals can take advantage of the discounted prices of tickets for these previews; second, you'll be able to hold off the critics until the production has had time to gel. The absolute last thing you need, especially on your first show, is for the critics to come out and review the production before it's ready. Audiences are known to be forgiving to young companies; critics are not.

During this time, you want to take the opportunity to learn from the audience what's working and what's not working about the show. The director will still be hanging around in the house, viewing the show and ironing out kinks. Sometimes a show's running time can simply be flat-out too long, and the director can only discover this by gauging the energy level of the audience. Remember that the people who make up your audiences are your bread and butter, and you must be acutely aware of their every need, their every response to your work. As with any business, if your new company is going to be successful, it must offer a service that patrons desire and enjoy.

During previews, the actors themselves should be encouraged to listen to their artistic instincts and to provide thoughtful feedback that will help to ensure the production's success. If there's a problem with a set, a costume, the lighting, etc., it's best that an actor bring it up during the previews instead of allowing it to affect the final production.

How I Learned (the Hard Way) to Speak Up

When I was cast to play the lead in Congo Square's production of *A Soldier's Play* by Charles Fuller, I was outfitted with a slightly oversized, ill-fitting costume. During our previews, I—and everyone else—could see that the costume wasn't working, yet none of us spoke up about it, and I continued to wear the uniform into the production's main run. Unfortunately, one person who *did* speak up about it was a critic, who made a point of mentioning the poor choice of garb in a published review of the show.

There must be a trust factor among the ensemble if you're going to succeed in this competitive profession. It doesn't matter if you're the artistic director or the most inexperienced actor in the ensemble; it's your responsibility to make sure that the work you put out as a team is as polished as it can be. You must be able to trust that the others in your ensemble will point out anything that might be "off"—and they must trust that you will do the same. A problem with a "minor" detail may seem like it's not worth mentioning, but it's those details that will separate your organization from the amateurs.

Critics

In general, everyone who's in the business of theater has a love-hate relationship with critics. If you're a producer and they give your show good reviews, you love them; they've stroked your ego and confirmed the worthiness of your endeavor—and their kind words may very well translate into more patrons. If you're an actor and the critics pan your performance, you hate them—not just because they're singling you out as the reason a show isn't working but also because any negative review may hurt your box office and harm the ensemble as a whole.

Love them or hate them, critics are an intricate part of the game and they should be respected. We were fortunate to receive great reviews of our first show, *The Piano Lesson*, from both the *Chicago Sun-Times* and the *Chicago Tribune*, as well as from smaller newspapers around town. This gave us an enormous burst of the confidence a young company desperately needs in order to carry on. We've also had a few less-than-glowing reviews. I can't deny that it's difficult to pick yourself up from a bad review. After putting so much time and energy in a production with little or no pay, oftentimes young organizations look to the critics for validation, and it can be heartbreaking when that validation isn't forthcoming.

However, keep in mind that you didn't form a theater company to please critics—you did so to please audiences and yourself. That's why you must have your *own aesthetic* and credo for evaluating your productions. Artists need to grow, and sometimes that means doing productions that challenge the ensemble artistically and that may or may not go over as well with audiences or critics. Theater companies young and old sometimes forget that they have to try things that will shake up the ensemble in order to make them grow as artists and that will prevent audiences from becoming tired of watching the same actor perform in the same "type" of play. As long as the ways in which you attempt to stretch fall within the guidelines of your company's overall aesthetic and mission, your theater will be able to bounce back from a bad review without any problems.

An artist usually can take a bad review in stride, but once in a while you might have a board member who overreacts to a negative review. This should be addressed immediately. Board members need to understand that your company is going to take some risks and that they must be prepared to handle it. Keep in mind that, unlike artists, many "civilians" who work regular nine-to-five jobs have learned to judge their own performance not by its intrinsic value but by the praise or criticism they receive from bosses and the marketplace. Boards of directors usually are made up of such civilians, so it's understandable that a board member might initially give a review a little more weight than you or one of your actors might.

Keep in mind, too, that positive reviews can sometimes be just as devastating as negative ones, for the simple reason that all the accolades can go to a young company's head. There are a million different personalities to manage in a theater company, so you can't allow yourself or anyone else's ego to get huge just from a couple of glowing reviews. Always remember this about your love-hate relationship with the critics: you're never as *good* as they say you are—and you're never as *bad* as they say you are, either.

Audience Assessments

Particularly during your first production, the marketing director should provide audience members with a survey to fill out after the show, to record their reaction to the performance, the ensemble, and the theater as a whole. This audience assessment should include space for the audience member to write down his or her contact information (name, address, telephone number, and e-mail address). Usually people are a bit reluctant to give out such personal information, but if you put on a great production, they're more likely to provide such details in order to be notified of upcoming plays, special events, discounted tickets, and the like. The assessment should also ask how the audience members heard about the production. Did they see an ad or read a blurb in the newspaper? Do they know one of the actors in the play? Are they alumni of the same college as the artistic director? This will help you figure out who's currently attending your shows and where you're getting the most bang for your advertising and marketing efforts.

Finally, audience members should be asked to write down any feedback they want to share about the production or their overall experience, as well as any suggestions on making your shows even more attractive to them. For example, you might ask, "What play or type of production would you like to see this company perform?" Of course, you'll get ridiculous suggestions that have absolutely nothing to do with your mission statement—but you'll also get a couple of gems that could start the wheels turning for your artistic director and your literary manager.

Play suggestions also make the people feel a part of the organization and its success. Think of the bond a patron would have with your company if you produced a production that he or she suggested. It's doubtful that a large LORT house would ever make such a major decision based on a suggestion by an audience member—but you most definitely can. In fact, this kind of "interactive" audience experience may be the wave of the future. Businesses the world over are soliciting feedback from their customers via the Internet; some car companies are even asking them to film online commercials for them.

Solicitations for feedback and suggestions need not be limited to in-theater surveys. Ask visitors to your Web site for ideas on how to improve both the site and the company, and invite them to sign up online to receive notifications of future events. Many small musical groups ensure they'll have audiences wherever they tour by tracking the fans who have signed onto the band's Web site, Facebook or MySpace page, and other such online venues and sending out online notices that the band is coming to town. Adding a survey, blog, or podcast to your own site could be another way of fostering loyal patrons. (See the sidebar in chapter 8 for more information on using blogs and podcasts to solicit feedback and connect with audiences.)

TALK-BACK NOTES

- Always offer as many previews you can afford. This will help both the performers and the director fine-tune the pace or rhythm of the production, endear the theater to audiences who take advantage of discounted preview tickets, and keep critics at bay until the production has had time to gel.

- Critics serve the general public, not the artists; their job is offer the community their opinions about the quality of the many events available to them. Remember that your company's success is determined not by the review of any particular critic, but by the degree to which you've achieved the goals of your mission statement.

- Surveys and other forms of audience assessments are absolutely vital if you're going to move your company forward and grow your audience. The more you know about them, the better you can service them.

11

LEADERSHIP

Ensuring Responsibility and Recognition

It's the sad truth that the performing arts are full of glory hounds and people with hidden agendas. There's really no way to make your organization 100 percent impervious to these kinds of people, but you can keep self-serving and destructive behavior to a minimum by creating a clear chain of command for your organization. If you know who's responsible for what, then you know who deserves praise and who doesn't. Along with this concept comes the simple issue of respect.

As a cofounder, you're probably going to be either the company's artistic director or its managing director. This means that you must have the maturity to supervise your peers and govern the organization with fairness and objectivity—tasks that are easier said than done. No matter what your intentions are, oftentimes an ensemble member may take offense at even the smallest decision you make for the company.

Personal Complications

To say that we had major arguments at Congo Square would be an understatement. Most companies do find themselves embroiled in internal strife from time to time; however, our battles were complicated by the fact that a few members of the ensemble (myself included) were dating each other. This is almost to be expected; members of a theater company spend an inordinate amount of time in one another's company, so relationships are bound to develop. Still, such relationships make the job of maintaining peace within the company that much harder—and the need for strict guidelines and an established chain of command that much more essential.

The cofounder's job is to set simple parameters by which the organization is to be run and managed. Set up rules that prohibit members from calling one another to discuss business after 7 P.M., require everyone to respect the authority of the artistic and managing directors and support their decisions even if a particular member disagrees with them, and mandate that no one ever leave a meeting with angry or upset feelings unresolved.

In the beginning stages of a young troupe, everyone is still a novice, so it's easy to second-guess one another. However, people should take comfort in the fact that, ultimately, it's the management, not the ensemble, who has to make—and be held accountable for—the tough decisions.

Accountability

The only way you're going to successfully launch your company is to make sure that, at every step, *someone is always responsible*. The fact that you've established a chain of command means zilch if you have a theater company full of people playing the blame game and constantly passing the buck. As a cofounder and a leader, you must hold yourself to the highest of standards, and you must hold your ensemble members to the same standards, as well. Theater is a dangerously competitive game, and the only way you're going to win is with discipline. If an ensemble member is responsible, as the marketing director, for writing up the press release and delivering it on time to the press, then it's your job to make sure that he or she gets the job done. That's not to say that you must micromanage people— you're going to have your hands full enough as it is—but in the early stages, you can't afford to let a single ball drop.

Accountability and an overriding sense of responsibility are what truly separate the winners from the losers. Keep in mind that we're all human and that many people will be working for no pay—but as my old coach used to say, "Excuses are like assholes; we all have one, and they all stink." The audience, critics, and funders don't care that you're waiting tables or working as a bartender, or that you're toiling behind the scenes on the company's arts-in-education program or Web site; they only care whether the show was any good. You're get just one shot to make this company work. It's the responsibility of everyone in the organization to comprehend that and to operate on all cylinders.

When I was the managing director of Congo Square, I insisted that our artistic director write up a production calendar for the entire season and that everyone in the organization treat it as the company road map. We met twice a month just to make sure that everyone was on the same page and to stay ahead of any problems that may have arisen during the previous two weeks. If someone missed a meeting, I simply treated that person as an adult, reminding him or her about the production calendar without hounding or lecturing.

Accountability is vital to the success of any organization. You can count on making a million mistakes during your first season, but if your company makes the *same* mistakes over and over again, you probably won't be in business for long. And you can't avoid repeating a problem if people don't own up to it. Accountability usually starts at the top—it's easier for the players to own up to their mistakes if the coach owns up to his. At Congo Square, I took the time to write job descriptions (and even solicited input on them from ensemble members) in order to ensure that every person would know *exactly* what was expected—what he or she was going to be held accountable for. It's important, as well, that everyone know what everyone else is doing during the run of a production. Remember, we're all temperamental artists, and we can be easily agitated if we believe we're doing the majority of the work because someone else isn't pulling his or her weight. By making everyone aware of everyone's job description (including those of both the artistic director and the managing director), there should be no question about whether or not any individual is doing his or her job.

As a leader, you can never afford to not hold people accountable for their actions (or lack of action), and you should never feel guilty asking anyone to contribute what's expected of him or her. I never had a problem asking people to strike a set, drop off a press release, perform telemarketing, work with the kids, clean the lobby, work the box office, understudy, inventory props, etc., simply because I had a million duties myself, not the least of which was raising money for the organization. Remember that, ultimately, the buck stops with the leaders of the company—so they must do everything they can to make sure that every aspect of that company is running the way it should be and that all members of the organization are doing their fair share.

Praise

At the same time that you hold people accountable for the work that they do (or don't do), you must always give credit where credit is due. This is particularly true in the case of people who are performing vital yet not very glamorous administrative tasks. The actors, directors, playwrights, and even the artistic director can overlook the important contributions of the many people working behind the scenes to make the magic happen.

Sometimes people think the term "credit" is a code word for "money." That is not the case. No one is going to get rich working in the nonprofit sector, so you have to find other ways to give your people credit and fulfill your ensemble's needs. Sometimes that may be in the form of a simple "thank you"; other times it can be expressed via an elaborate end-of-season party. However you do it, it's your job to keep your people motivated and working. I think it's a good idea for the company to not produce over the summer so that your ensemble members have some time to catch their breaths. And summertime is a good time to check in with yourself on a personal level and honestly ask yourself whether you're willing to give this kind of effort every year. Everyone in the organization should take a well deserved vacation and come back fully reloaded.

At the end of your first successful season, it's a good idea to reflect on the fact that your success probably couldn't have happened without an active board of directors. Just as the ensemble is composed of people with vastly different personalities, the board is made up of unique individuals, as well. Some board members may be more charismatic than others, but you must make it a point to acknowledge *every* board member's contributions.

Finding things to praise and acknowledge about each and every member of your organization while, at the same time, keeping a vigilant eye out for glory hounds is sometimes easier said than done, but it's important. The last thing you want is to lose a hardworking, valuable board member, ensemble member, or volunteer simply because he or she feels underappreciated.

TALK-BACK NOTES

- Accountability is the ultimate test for any business. As the founder, you must create a culture in which people welcome the fact that they are held accountable for their job performance.

- Along with holding people accountable, you must also recognize and compliment the good work they do. Remember: it never hurts to praise hardworking individuals for a job well done.

12

IDENTITY

Congo Square's
First Season

So far we've focused our attention on setting up a plan of operation that gives your company the best possible chance of survival during its crucial first year. In the next three chapters, we'll examine to what extent an actual theater company—Congo Square—was able to put that plan into practice as it mounted the productions of its first three seasons. With luck, after reading about our experiences with both preproduction and the postproduction wrap-up, you'll be able to learn from some of our mistakes and avoid some of the problems we faced as a new organization (don't worry; you'll still face plenty of your own!). The information in these chapters will also give you insight into how stressful running an organization can be, particularly when money is low and tempers are high. Finally, you'll get to see why we were so successful right out of the gate.

We begin with Congo Square's inaugural season, in which we laid the crucial groundwork for our success by establishing a strong sense of identity for Congo Square. For any theater company, this clear vision is absolutely essential to landing on the community's radar. The plays you choose your first season will define and place you in a particular category. This is precisely what you want because funders need to know exactly who they're giving money to. If you don't have a good sense of your place in the community and the industry, it will be obvious.

In addition to cultivating a strong sense of identity, we also took care to heed the advice of our advisory board members, and pursued a number of marketing tactics, such as creating an inviting Web site, giving away eye-catching T-shirts, and telemarketing, most of which paid off big time. Our selection of which plays to perform—and when in the year to perform them—also contributed to the company's success. Believe it or not, some plays work better in the fall than in the spring or summer. After reading this chapter you'll have a better idea of why that is.

Fall

Preproduction

To every red-blooded American, autumn can only mean two things: the start of football season and the kickoff of theater season. I strongly recommend that you launch your first production in the fall, when theater patrons are eager to take in new plays and performances. Newspapers across the nation hype previews of autumn films, operas, concerts, and, of course, theater productions. However, long before you can make yourself part of the hype machine and battle your way to the front page of the arts section of your local newspaper, you and the other members of the ensemble must decide which plays you will produce during your inaugural season. These plays will define who you are to the public—and they can make or break you. You only get one chance to make a first impression, so the productions that you and your comrades decide on had better be on point.

The first play, which should be produced in the fall (roughly between September and November), should be the biggest and most exciting of the three you will launch that year. You want to put points on the scoreboard early in order to let the public know you're now officially in the game. The play should showcase your best actors, designers, and director. It must epitomize your mission statement and give people an idea of what you have to offer down the road. Oh, and it should be phenomenal!

The first production we performed was August Wilson's *The Piano Lesson*. We mounted it at the Chicago Dramatists Theatre, a small, 66-seat house, and I'm proud to say it was both a critical and a box office smash. For that production we hired a great Chicago-based director named Ron OJ Parson, who had been the artistic director of his own theater company called the Onyx Theatre Ensemble of Chicago and who had directed plays all over the country.

It's a good idea to not bite off more than you can chew in your first season. If no one in your ensemble is a playwright, don't suddenly decide to have someone write a play. Also, always beware of the "news": don't open a *new* play in a *new* space as a *new* company. Too many *new*s! As a *new* company, we selected an *established* space to house our first production—a space that audiences were already used to patronizing. Now we needed a *recognized* play. During that time in Chicago, many of the theaters were focusing on developing new black playwrights; we set ourselves apart by returning to the classic black plays and playwrights we had studied in school.

Allocating Your Available Funds

I recommend that you spend most of your available funds on the *first* play of the inaugural season. Most of this money will be spent on marketing in order to ensure that both it and your new company receive some notice. Your second production of the season should be allocated a smaller amount of money, and the third should be allocated the least amount.

As we debated about what our inaugural show should be, I came up with the idea of doing *The Piano Lesson*. The hook was that the play hadn't been performed in Chicago in 10 years, and that the Pulitzer Prize–winning drama would be celebrating its 10th anniversary in 2000, the year of our first season. So here we were, a start-up company setting out on this huge undertaking of producing a major play by a major playwright at a well-known space. It was a daring move, and the local media ate it up.

As a new, untested theater company, we had to create hype and buzz in an already saturated market. We couldn't compete, in terms of sheer spectacle, with the likes of Chicago's Goodman Theatre (which normally produces works by Mr. Wilson), but we definitely could hype the quality of our ensemble's acting chops. When just starting out in the business, always, *always* focus on the plain old nuts and bolts of acting instead of great stage effects and other such gimmicks. Let the big boys do *Star Wars* and *Jaws*; you do *Taxi Driver* and *The Godfather*. Audiences the world over realize there's nothing greater than watching a hungry actor feast on a scrumptious script. In the beginning, that's the only thing you have to offer them, and that's exactly what you should serve—on a silver platter.

The Piano Lesson by August Wilson

Synopsis: This Pulitzer Prize–winning drama deals with a family's haunting legacy surrounding a prized piano.

Directed by Ron OJ Parson
Set Design by Patrick Kerwin
Lighting Design by Kathy Perkins
Costume Design by McKinley Johnson
Sound Design by Larry Vance
Stage Manager: Adero Fleming

Featuring: Aaron Todd Douglas, Libya Pugh, Derrick Sanders, Will Sims II, Ann Joseph, Charles Michael Moore, J. J. McCormick, Amber Dorbin, and Lanisha Yates.

Postproduction

At the end of the run of every show you produce, your company should always hold two postproduction wrap-ups in order to properly determine the success or failure of the production. The board of directors should hold its own postproduction wrap-up to discuss ways to improve fundraising and fiscal management, while the ensemble conferences to examine every aspect of the production from an artistic point of view. Everything and everyone should be put up for evaluation, from the artistic and managing directors, marketing director, actors, director, designers, and other people who had a hand in the play to the work's sets, costumes, lighting, and other features. Both praise and constructive criticism should be given where they are due.

In addition, this is when you decide whether or not you're going to continue to work with certain designers or actors again. We had auditioned and were blessed to have two older actors, J. J. McCormick and the late Charles Michael Moore, work with us in our first endeavor. Each man brought a level of depth and experience to his character that anchored the production, and everyone in the ensemble immediately agreed that we wanted to work with them again in the future. (Charles would, the following year, portray my "abusive" father in our production of the hilarious comedy *Playboy of the West Indies*.) However, because of the constant delays we'd experienced in regard to the construction of the set (parts of which were still being put together the day of *opening night*), we vowed never to work with the set designer again. Despite the fact that he was an enormous talent and that he'd been forced to work on a shoestring budget, we concluded that it was better for everyone's sanity that we not collaborate again.

We were most fortunate to receive glowing reviews after *The Piano Lesson*. We were especially gratified by the review that was published in the *Chicago Tribune*; the critic astutely understood what we were trying to accomplish with Congo Square. Getting a review such as that is akin to having someone writing your company a blank check: it's your responsibility to take it to the local foundations and "cash" it by using it to secure more funding for your company. Immediately after the enormous success of *The Piano Lesson* we received a $30,000 grant from the Argos Foundation, based on an application that I and Ann Joseph had written. With funds now secured for our next season, it became official: Congo Square Theatre Company was in business. We immediately set about figuring out what we could do to improve the company in time for our next production.

Winter

Preproduction

Your winter play, which should run roughly between January and March, can be a little more daring than the fall piece. For our winter production, we performed the Chicago premiere of *Before It Hits Home* by Cheryl West, also at the Chicago Dramatists Theatre. This play deals with the subjects of AIDS and bisexuality in the black community, and our production of it turned out to be another box office and critical hit.

Most of us had become familiar with the play while we were in school, and we were shocked to realize that no other theater in the city had yet performed it. We leaped at the chance! Premieres and anniversary productions are *hooks* that both the media and audiences love. If you have an opportunity to do a local premiere of an established play, take it. It's easier to promote—and the easier it is to promote, the better chance you have of putting butts in the seats. Due to the play's subject matter, we focused our promotional efforts on the gay black community in Chicago, a previously untapped theater market.

The play was another actor's piece that showcased different members of our ensemble. The purpose of your second production is to hit audiences in the gut (or between the eyes), if only to let them know that you are "for real." With *Before It Hits Home*, we did just that: night after night, by the end of the play there wasn't a dry eye in the house.

Before It Hits Home by Cheryl L. West

Synopsis: A young bisexual musician must confront his family when he acquires AIDS.

Directed by Anthony Amiri Edwards
Set and Lighting Design by Logan Shunmugam
Sound Design by Larry Nance
Stage Manager: Rudolph Wallace Jr.
Assistant Stage Manager: Adero Fleming

Featuring: Javon Johnson, Aaron Todd Douglas, Monifa Days, Willie B. Goodson, Min-aha Beeck, Will Sims II, TaRon Patton, Ira Carol McGill, Andrea Salloum, Leonard Wilson, and Jemelle Lloyd.

Postproduction

After its second touchdown with *Before It Hits Home*, our company was feeling pretty good about itself. We'd produced another critical and box office hit; one that shined a much-needed light on a taboo subject in the black community. We'd been able to raise both money and awareness for AIDS research and genuinely endear ourselves to the public. However, we still faced challenges as a new organization, not the least of which was figuring out how to pay our actors. After each performance of our first production, *The Piano Lesson*, Derrick had introduced himself and explained to the audience that the actors were working without pay and that any donation to them would be greatly appreciated. Then Derrick and another ensemble member, Will Sims II, would collect the money and divide it among the cast. We soon discovered, however, that while walking away with a few dollars in their pockets after a performance may have made the actors feel good, this practice was a big mistake! It created tension between the artists and the administrators, who received nothing. Remember, it takes just as much (if not more) effort to perform behind the scenes—raising funds, managing the box office, doing marketing, etc.—as it does to perform onstage. By agreeing to pay your *actors* to perform without compensating the *administrators*, you're sending up a big red flag that announces (erroneously or not) what is *really* important to the organization. Worse, you end up rewarding that ensemble member who loves to act but who refuses to work behind the scenes, while the members of your ensemble who work their butts off making sure all the vital administrative tasks are accomplished go unrewarded and unrecognized.

Amiri Edwards, the director of *Before It Hits Home* and a founding Congo Square board member, brought this problem to my attention, as well as the fact that it was simply not good public relations to have your artistic director literally begging audiences for money after they've already paid the admission price. At the next board meeting, we voted to put an end to the practice. Our young board decided that it was inappropriate to solicit donations in this way, particularly in light of the sensitive subject matter of the show. Instead, we decided to pay all ensemble members a small stipend for the entire run of the show. This way, regardless of whether the show sold out or flopped each night, the actors were at least guaranteed *some* money. It seemed like a reasonable compromise—but it didn't go down very well with a few of the ensemble members, who thought that the board might have overstepped its bounds.

As a founder of the theater company, it's extremely important to communicate with both the board of directors and the ensemble of artists, because your job is to make certain things run smoothly between the two. One can't survive without the other if the organization's going to have any chance at launching successfully.

During our run of *Before It Hits Home*, we were faced with yet another fact of life in the theater world. Once a director leaves a production after opening night, it becomes the stage manager's job to maintain the director's vision and the integrity of the piece. Unfortunately, if a stage manager lets them get away with it, some actors can find themselves flirting with melodrama and end up pandering to an audience.

In one scene of *Before It Hits Home*, the character Wendal slowly realizes that he may have infected his pregnant girlfriend with the virus as a result of cheating on her with a man. It is an extremely difficult scene to perform and the actor must handle it very delicately; otherwise, it's easy to go overboard in terms of the level of emotion, and that lets the audience off the hook. I believe that happened in our production from time to time, especially as we neared the end of the run: the actors' performances became a tad too melodramatic, and the result was that the audience didn't have the same gut-wrenching experience that previous audiences had. We definitely made sure to address that issue during the show's postproduction critique.

Possibly the greatest thing about our second show was that through it, we acquired a talented and enthusiastic new ensemble member, TaRon Patton. Here was an actress who not only relished her role onstage but also volunteered to help the young company in any way she could. After the production closed, the ensemble immediately voted to make her a part of the organization. If you're lucky enough to discover potential new members for your organization, test their loyalty by assigning them tasks that will help you mount a successful production. Of course everyone wants to be *on* the stage—but during the start-up phase of your company, what you really need are more people who are willing to roll up their sleeves and help you *build* it.

Spring

Preproduction

The last production of your first season (which should run roughly between April and June) is basically a test. It allows you to see if you've developed a kernel of a fan base—and to see if you and your comrades can keep up your level of intensity without killing one another. Show business is not for the thin skinned, and the stress levels of building a company can be astronomically high, particularly in the start-up stage. By your third show, you and the other members of the ensemble should have at least some idea as to whether or not you can continue, and want to continue, on your chosen path.

Not every start-up company produces three shows a season, but there are many benefits to doing so. By the time your third production reaches its end, you should have in place a firmly established ritual for managing people and any problems that arise. In addition, you should have enough financial data to judge the success of the company from a monetary standpoint. It's difficult to do that with only two shows under your belt—and by producing three shows each season, you give yourself a buffer to ride things out in the event that one of the productions flops.

A third production also gives you an opportunity to correct some of the mistakes you made with the previous two productions, and since it's the smallest and least expensive of the season's three shows, it may also give you an opportunity to allow an ensemble member to make his or her directing debut. It's tough enough to break into mainstream theater as an actor, but as a director? Forget about it. With your own company, however, you and other ensemble members can begin to hone those directing skills. And who knows? Maybe one day you'll get a call inviting you to direct a show for one of the big boys. Stranger things have certainly happened.

Another excellent reason to produce three productions is that it gives the potential board members you've identified in the community three opportunities to see your company and ensemble of actors in action. Nothing—and I do mean *nothing*—convinces an individual to join your association more than a stellar performance. In addition, the third show helps to solidify your brand in the psyche of the community and serves to reassure your audiences that your new company is here to stay.

The final production of Congo Square's inaugural season was the South African classic *The Island* by Athol Fugard, John Kani, and Winston Ntshona. We performed this two-man show at the Chicago Cultural Center in downtown Chicago. Due to the play's political theme, we wanted to be near an audience that would appreciate the message of the drama. The cultural center was also a cheap space to rent, and it came complete with its own patrons and infrastructure, including a marketing program.

The Island by Athol Fugard, John Kani, and Winston Ntshona

Synopsis: Two South African political prisoners decide to perform the Greek Tragedy *Antigone* during apartheid.

Directed by Derrick Sanders
Lighting and Set Design by Logan Shunmugam
Sound Design by Larry Nance

Featuring: Reginald Nelson and Will Sims II

Postproduction

Although *The Island* was a critical success and was even attended by our mentor August Wilson, it certainly wasn't a box office triumph. We had a low turnout of patrons compared to the other two shows—but because the venue was extremely cheap to rent and the show involved minimal production costs, the play didn't break us. However, Derrick and I did have our first real major battle during this production, and it involved both artistic and managerial issues. This was Derrick's directorial debut, and both Will and I believed that he had a *long* way to go in terms of how he communicated with actors. Whenever an actor did something he didn't like during rehearsals, you'd have thought the sky was falling. This made for some heated arguments among the three of us throughout the process and a pretty poor creative environment. Granted, we all were under pressure: we had a limited amount of time in which to mount the show and we were all working full-time paying jobs and trying to raise money for the company at the same time. In addition, Will had just discovered that his wife was pregnant.

It didn't help that the three of us felt somewhat neglected because other ensemble members had taken acting jobs at other theaters instead of working behind the scenes to ensure that the final production of the season was a success. As a result of people putting their acting careers ahead of the good of the company, the marketing of the show, in particular, suffered, and that contributed to our poor box office. It takes the entire ensemble's participation to distribute the posters and postcards, place the advertising, send out the press releases, make the phone calls, and send the e-mails that are required in order to get audiences into the theater. One or two people can't handle it; marketing (especially in the start-up stage) is *everyone's* responsibility, and each person must handle his or her fair share of the burden. Without the hard work of each ensemble member, the hype machine can't work efficiently or effectively.

The next major battle that Derrick and I had during the production of this show was about *money*. Derrick believed that he should be paid for both directing and costume design because he'd done the "work" of finding Will and me some khaki shorts and shirts to wear as costumes. My argument was that, as the company's cofounder and artistic director, his first priority should be to help save the company money instead of looking for reasons to take from the pot. He adamantly disagreed, and the tension between us reached epic proportions. Eventually the acting managing director, Amiri, decided to intervene and give Derrick a fee for his work as the show's costume designer. Amiri's thoughts were that since Derrick *had* done the work and since we had, in fact, budgeted some funds to pay a costume designer, it was best to just give him the money. As much as I hate to admit, it was a bitter pill for me to swallow, and I'm positive that the whole ordeal affected my working relationship as an actor with Derrick, the director. After *The Island* proved to be a box office disappointment, I couldn't help but think that if we had not paid the artistic director a costume designer fee, *The Island's* numbers would have looked at least a little better than they did. The saying "a penny saved is a penny earned" holds true not only in personal finance but in the nonprofit sector as well. In order to ensure your best possible chance of surviving your first season, it truly is imperative that every member of the company knows that sacrifices—of time, energy, and, yes, *money*—will simply have to be made.

The first season was finally over—and despite our many arguments and death threats, we all knew we had created something special. We also knew that although summer was now upon us, soon enough it would be fall and we'd have to try to do it all over again.

TALK-BACK NOTES

- Beware of taking on too many "news" at the same time: you can't be a new company performing a new play in a new venue.

- Young companies are well served by marketing "hooks" that help to establish your brand. Two such hooks are premieres and anniversary productions, which serve as excellent vehicles for getting face time with the local media and stimulating buzz.

- If you're going to give your actors stipends for their work onstage, also give stipends to the people who carry out the behind-the-scenes and front-of-house tasks in order to avoid brewing resentment.

- There are many advantages to producing three shows in a season instead of just two, particularly in the case of a young company that is trying to find its footing.

13

CONSISTENCY

Congo Square's
Second Season

The second season will probably be the hardest, because you'll be desperately trying to avoid the sophomore jinx. Consistency is what you're striving to achieve: you want to prove to your audiences, the media, other theater companies, and the philanthropic community that your first season was not beginner's luck but the realization of a well-executed plan. The overall focus of your second season should be on marketing your company and identifying your patrons. By this time, you will have accumulated enough data and contact information from the audiences of the previous three productions to start analyzing that information and putting it to use. You want to start planning strategies to attract niche groups, such as women, sports fans, academics, and so forth, to your productions. And you should capitalize on the success of your first season to get your board more involved in fundraising and other endeavors.

Consistency also relates to staying true to your mission statement—refraining from suddenly skidding out of your chosen lane. The productions we chose for our second season were the perfect embodiment of what we'd set out to accomplish from the beginning: the production of theater from the African diaspora. We'd started, in year one, with the work of a well-known, Pulitzer Prize–winning playwright, the Chicago premiere of a social drama, and a political piece about South Africa. In year two, we built on the identity we'd established by producing another Chicago premiere, a powerful women's piece, and a Caribbean comedy that was adapted from an Irish classic. By offering our community this diverse selection of material, we remained true to our mission statement and continued to impress audiences and critics, which strengthened their support.

The key to staying true to your mission is to make sure that the ensemble is involved in the play selection process. If someone is extremely passionate about a play, and it works within the parameters of your mission statement, trust that person's instincts and mount the production. Derrick and I learned about trusting the judgment of our ensemble members in regard to choosing material, and it paid off big time.

Fall

Preproduction

As Congo Square entered fall 2001, we were as determined as ever to build on the enormous momentum we had acquired the previous year. Over the summer we'd held our first annual "Juneteenth" fundraiser, at which we raised a modest $2,700 in extra cash for the company, and we'd moved our organization's headquarters from my apartment to Union Park on Chicago's West Side. There, we became involved in the Chicago Park District's Arts Partners in Residence program, a program that unites artists and communities in Chicago parks. In exchange for office space, we agreed to provide theater classes to the community. Arts Partners in Residence is a great program, and it's one of the many reasons Chicago is known as "the city that works." I heard about the program from Roxanne Ward, a former head of the park district. Dina Rutledge was the park supervisor at Union Park, and she and her staff welcomed us with open arms.

With our new administrative office in place, the company could now comfortably execute another plan of attack. The best decision we made coming into the second season was to mount all three productions at the same location. The company had earned enough money from the previous season's box office and grants to make a down payment on rental space for all three shows at the Chicago Dramatists Theatre. No longer burdened with trying to market different venues, we could now hype our "home"—and, ultimately, see if we could secure a loyal fan base.

To open the season, we chose a knockout of a production: the Chicago premiere of *Ali* by Geoffrey C. Ewing and Graydon Royce. The play had come to my attention the previous year when I was understudying in August Wilson's *King Hedley II* at the Goodman. I'd spoken to the late actor Charlie Brown about finding a play for our next season, and he suggested *Ali*. I read it and was floored by the work, as was the entire ensemble.

Ali by Geoffrey C. Ewing and Graydon Royce

Synopsis: A two-man Chicago premiere about the life and times of the greatest athlete of the 20th century.

Directed by Ron OJ Parson and Derrick Sanders
Set Design by Robert Martin
Lighting Design by Logan Shunmugam

Featuring: Javon Johnson and Ron OJ Parson

Postproduction

Success is often simply a matter of timing, and 2001 was the perfect time to do this show. ESPN, *Sports Illustrated*, *Esquire*, and *GQ* were all counting down their versions of the "100 Best Athletes of the 20th Century," and Muhammad Ali topped almost everyone's list. He was also the subject of a soon-to-be-released big-budget biopic starring Will Smith. And Ali himself had ties to the area—during the height of his career, he actually lived in Chicago for a period of time. The man has the most recognizable face on the planet, and playwrights Geoffrey C. Ewing and Graydon Royce did a phenomenal job of capturing the legacy of this cultural icon. In short, promoting a show about Muhammad Ali in a sports-crazed town like Chicago was about as difficult as busting a grape in a fruit fight. The lesson? A good producer always, always know his or her market!

Ensemble member Javon Johnson played younger Ali, and director Ron OJ Parson portrayed the fighter in his later years. Each man was on his A game and performed exceptional work. The play is an emotional piece that confronts issues such as religious freedom, war, and patriotism. The connection was not lost on us when during the show's run, the United States fell victim to the September 11 terrorist attacks. The attacks dealt businesses all over the country a major blow, and Chicago theaters were no exception. However, as many of our fellow companies struggled to woo back patrons after the attacks, word of mouth about our production was so powerful and its themes were so timely that audiences continued to show up at our box office.

Once again, our philosophy of consulting mentors (actor Charlie Brown in this case) paid off big time. Thanks to Charlie's suggestion, we had come up with another knockout production.

Winter

Preproduction

While *Ali* triumphantly showcased the male members of our ensemble, our female members waited patiently in the wings, eager to score their own success with our next play. *From the Mississippi Delta*, by Endesha Ida Mae Holland, was one of the plays that hadn't make the cut for our first season. It had been suggested by Libya Pugh (who was, hands down, our most passionate and talented ensemble member at the time), and the only reason we decided against it that first year was that no one else in the organization had heard of it. In our minds, the inaugural season was better served by familiar plays, and *Mississippi Delta* didn't fit the bill.

Bills change, however, and as part of our second season, we wanted to spread our wings a bit and produce an exemplary play that might not be so familiar to audiences. The minute we began the selection process, Libya suggested we reconsider *From the Mississippi Delta*. We still had our doubts, but Libya was insistent, and this time no one in the ensemble had the energy to argue with her. To be honest, we thought we were doing her a favor by agreeing to produce the play. After all, the men were going to shine in *Ali*; why not give the women an opportunity to shine as well?

As it turned out, not only was the production an acting tour de force for the three women (Libya Pugh, Ann Joseph, and TaRon Patton), but *From the Mississippi Delta* would go on to break Congo Square box office records, surpassing those of both *Ali* and *The Piano Lesson*. Female patrons came in droves to see that production. After catching a performance, Martha Lavey, the artistic director of Steppenwolf Theatre Company, became convinced that the women of our ensemble were the *true* talent behind the success of Congo Square. She was, of course, correct; I just didn't realize it at the time.

From the Mississippi Delta
by Dr. Endesha Ida Mae Holland

Synopsis: Dr. Holland's riveting coming-of-age story of growing up poor and black in Mississippi.

Directed by Cheryl Lynn Bruce
Lighting Design by Kathy Perkins
Set Design by Logan Shunmugam
Costume Design by Christine E. Pascual
Stage Manager: I. Stefanie Foster

Featuring Libya Pugh, Ann Joseph, and TaRon Patton

Postproduction

We all learned a valuable lesson with *From the Mississippi Delta*: there is no substitute for passion. Libya's passion for this play was all consuming—and, boy, did it pay off, both artistically and financially. Derrick and I both had totally underestimated the power of the female audience; thank God we learned this lesson early. There's a reason Oprah Winfrey has more money than the Queen of England—she gives voice to millions of women who otherwise have none. Keep in mind that this play was performed during February in Chicago—yet the people didn't let the harsh winter deter them from trudging to our doorstep to see this show. All three of the actresses gave brilliant performances, and Libya went on to be recognized by the *Chicago Sun-Times* as one of the top 10 actresses in Chicago that year, an honor that was largely due to her performance in *From the Mississippi Delta*. Also instrumental to that play's success was its director, Cheryl Lynn Bruce, a veteran actress who had originated one of the roles in the national premiere of the play. She brought an earthy, nontraditional approach to the rehearsal process that frustrated the actors but nevertheless got the job done.

However, maybe the single greatest thing about our experience with *From the Mississippi Delta* was that after this production, advisory board members Les Coney and Roxanne Ward finally decided to officially come onto Congo Square's board of directors. Their levels of expertise and connections in the civic community were enormous, and when they joined our board it was a huge score for the organization.

Spring

Preproduction

The five plays we'd produced so far had all been dramas. They'd served us well and with the singular exception of *The Island*, all had been box office successes. Now it was time for us to do a comedy. We settled on *Playboy of the West Indies* by Mustapha Matura. It was an adaptation of the Irish classic *The Playboy of the Western World* by J. M. Synge.

Our play selection process lasted from late November through mid-March. During that time, the ensemble would gather over at my house on Sunday or Monday nights and read the plays that were under consideration. Each ensemble member brought two plays to be considered, and after we'd each read them, we narrowed the choices to the final five, which we read aloud as a group. After the staged readings of all five plays, the artistic director then chose three for the upcoming season. Due to the heavy West Indian dialect featured in *Playboy*, we almost passed on the play. Rather than having actors fake an accent, the playwright actually wrote the piece in his native Trinidadian vernacular. It was a *long* night trying to get through it, but in the end, the ensemble all felt we were up to the challenge of mounting such a production.

The play hadn't been performed in Chicago since its world premiere in 1988, and it fit perfectly with our mission statement. It was a large, ambitious production, and it wouldn't have happened had we not recruited two veterans who'd been part of the 1988 production. Our advisory board member Chuck Smith agreed to direct, and the charismatic, ebullient actor Ernest Perry Jr. signed on to star. Coming off the huge surprise success of *From the Mississippi Delta*, we were going to need all the help we could get.

Playboy of the West Indies by Mustapha Matura

Synopsis: This warm, hilarious comedy is adapted from an Irish classic, infused with a calypso beat, and set on the sunny island of Trinidad.

Directed by Chuck Smith
Set and Lighting Design by Logan Shunmugam
Costume Design by Christine E. Pascual
Sound Design by Matt Ulm
Stage Manger: Adero Fleming
Assistant Stage Manager: Sydney D. Chatman
Cultural Advisor: Raul S. Cambridge

Featuring: Ann Joseph, Reginald Nelson, Derrick Sanders, TaRon Patton, Charles Michael Moore, Tusiime Jackson, Tabitha Cross, Daryl Satcher, Jaimie Turner and Ernest Perry Jr.

Postproduction

Playboy was the slam dunk on a stellar second season. We had finally gelled as an organization. Unlike the previous year, when actors from the ensemble found work at other theaters, leaving other members high and dry to handle the administration duties alone, everyone rallied around this warm production and made it a success. Ensemble member Aaron Todd Douglas even helped the set designer, Logan, build the rum shop where the action took place.

There isn't a huge West Indian population in Chicago, so the production lived up to our mission statement by transporting audiences to an unfamiliar location and exposing them to a unique culture. What makes me so proud about _Playboy of_

the West Indies is that the company met the challenge of producing such a work head on. None of us knew much about the
West Indies or its culture, but that didn't discourage us. As
luck would have it, our Web designer, Jeff Trimmingham, was
originally from Trinidad; when I told him we needed a dialect coach, he recommended Raul Cambridge, a West Indian
renaissance man.

The board of directors was on its A game as well, once
Les Coney and Roxanne Ward had agreed to officially come
on board as president and vice-president. The board sponsored
the show's opening night, selling tickets to the event for as
much as $50 a person. In attendance that night were some of
the top movers and shakers of Chicago's civic community, and
the company made so much money on opening night that the
play could have bombed during the rest of its run and we still
would have been fine financially. That's one of the reasons it's
so crucial to have a good board of directors that understands
the importance of raising money for the organization. Your
job is to make it easier for board members to raise that money
by doing exceptional work.

During its second season, Congo Square also built on the
success of the previous year by putting the audience database
to good use and marketing our new production to previous
patrons via telephone calls and e-mails. Initially, some ensemble members where skeptical about soliciting people in this
manner, but I reminded them that these patrons had given
us their contact information precisely because they *wanted* to
be contacted. Theater is just like any other business; without
loyal customers who patronize an establishment time and time
again, it's unlikely that the establishment will stay afloat very
long.

Ultimately, *Playboy of the West Indies* was such a major success because of the fact that Chuck Smith decided to direct it and Ernest Perry Jr. agreed to star in it. As August Wilson always told us, *"When people offer their help, call them on it."* These two theater powerhouses helped us to close out our second season with a resounding bang.

TALK-BACK NOTES

- For the second season, plan to produce all three productions in one venue so that audiences become accustomed to coming to the same space. This allows you to build a loyal fan base, which will eventually result in loyal subscribers.

- Successful theater companies thrive because they know what kinds of subjects and issues their audiences desire to see plays about.

- Now is the time to put your young board of directors to a test by having them host a fundraising gala for the opening night of the last production of the year.

14

HUBRIS

Congo Square's
Third Season

By season three, you pretty much know what you're doing and you have a good idea of what makes a hit production. If you're fortunate enough to have lasted for two seasons and to have received great reviews, the thing you must now fight against, more than anything else, is *hubris*. Every successful person has a certain level of confidence in his or her abilities and talent; however, there's a fine line between confidence and cockiness. After two extremely successful seasons, all of our hard work had paid off and we were now the talk of Chicago theater. All the top critics in the major local newspapers loved us, and the name "Congo Square" was quickly moving through the city's philanthropic community as well. All of this attention began to cloud our judgment and, as a result, we made some boneheaded errors in season three.

Once you achieve a degree of success in the theater, the essential point to consider is that you can't patent a formula that allows you to maintain that success simply by doing the same things you did before. The theater is a living, breathing organism that continues to grow even while you're sleeping or working behind a bar, and what worked one year may be disastrous in the next. You can't stand still, you can't rest on your laurels, and you certainly can't kid yourself that you've got it all figured out and can coast from here on. In order to keep up with a growing, living, changing entity, you have to continue to grow yourself. In the third season of our company's existence, we learned that the hard way.

Fall

Preproduction

Congo Square entered fall 2002 with the largest financial surplus we had seen to date. In two years, we'd gone from having a production budget of $10,000 for *The Piano Lesson* to a budget of $65,000 for *A Soldier's Play*. The board membership fee went from $300 to $1,000, and we received so much money from local foundations that we were now able to pay modest fees to the artistic and managing directors, the production manager, the director of development, and others. I'm extremely proud to say that in our second season, we actually earned more on our box office (around $48,000 for all three productions) than we received in contributions and grants (around $35,000). That is unheard of in a young theater company, which usually receives more in donated funds than in earned income. It was because of this success that the company decided to mount an ambitious production of Charles Fuller's Pulitzer Prize–winning drama *A Soldier's Play*. It was a risky and expensive venture, not only because of the large cast that would be involved but also because we decided to change our venue from the Chicago Dramatists Theatre to Theatre Building Chicago.

Theatre Building Chicago has a long, illustrious history, and it has hosted many of Chicago's best troupes over the years. It's a very high-profile venue, and it was celebrating its 25th anniversary when we were there. The rent was expensive—at around $1,100 a week, it was nearly double the rent we'd been paying at the Chicago Dramatists Theatre. However, unlike Chicago Dramatists Theatre, Theatre Building Chicago ran the box office for its tenants. As I stated earlier, the management of the box office can be a pain during the launching of a company. Many patrons want to purchase their tickets with credit cards; a lot of them prefer to order tickets online. These were services we simply couldn't offer at the beginning. We were strictly a "cash only, pay at the door" operation. Now, with Theatre Building Chicago's staff and vast resources at our disposal, we could offer advance ticket sales online and accommodate credit card purchases at the door. In addition, it was a larger house; at 120 seats, the capacity was almost double that of our old space at the Dramatists Theatre—and with our new tickets price of $25, we believed we'd positioned Congo Square to make a nice amount of money from this play. We also had Chuck Smith on board again to direct the production.

With a comfortable financial cushion, two new, visionary board members, a respected and talented director, a Pulitzer Prize–winning play, and a larger, well-known venue, we were sure that all we had to do was sit back and let the machine work its magic. We were wrong.

A Soldier's Play by Charles Fuller

Synopsis: In 1944 Louisiana a black sergeant is murdered, and Captain Davenport, the army's first black commissioned officer, has been sent in to investigate.

Directed by Chuck Smith
Set and Lighting Design by Logan Shunmugam
Costume Design by Christine E. Pascual
Assistant Director: Geoffrey Scott
Stage Manager: Sydney D. Chatman
Assistant Stage Manager: Natalie McKnight
Prop Mistress: Debra Irving
Sound Designer: Matthew Ulm
Sound Technician: Vijah Joshi

Featuring: E. Milton Wheeler, Tim Miller, Leonard House Jr. Derrick Sanders, Daryl Satcher, Damani Singleton, Rolando A. Boyce Sr., Willie B. Goodson, Reginald Nelson, Warren Jackson, Will Sims II, Karl Hamilton, and Dan Wolfe.

Postproduction

An old retired professor at the University of Illinois by the name of Hobgood once told me, "Always read reviews *after* a show closes." Now I know why. Up until this point, we would all read the reviews the moment they hit the streets, and sometimes we even checked the Internet to see what the critics had to say online. We valued and trusted their opinions more than we cared to admit, and sometimes that backfired on us. I was a little devastated, on a few levels, by the reviews *A Soldier's Play* received. As an actor, I was crushed to read that I was "dragging down the show," and, as the company's managing director, I sure as hell didn't like the fact that at least one critic asked audiences to "give this one a few days" before buying a ticket. Our production of *A Soldier's Play* was an expensive show at an expensive venue, and we needed those ticket sales *now*!

In retrospect, I think the critics were pretty fair and objective in their reviews of both my performance and the show as a whole. As the lead in a production, it's your job to drive the truck and keep the show moving. I knew I wasn't at my best on opening night, and I worked diligently to improve night after night, but I didn't really hit full stride until the last couple of weeks of the run. What's more, my "managing director" hat was never far from my head, and my worries about the extent to which my performance was affecting ticket sales hindered my ability to focus on doing my job as an actor. It's a dilemma that's faced by members of any young organization: each person must take on a number of roles, and it's easy to let one role affect another.

The production also didn't do as well as we'd hoped it would because we eased up on our group sales initiative. For previous productions, we'd sold tickets in advance to church groups, alumni associations, fraternities and sororities, and local businesses. Oftentimes, it is group sales that determine whether a production is a box office hit or flop. The only thing that really saved *A Soldier's Play* from total financial disaster was the huge opening night gala that board member Les Coney threw; during that event we were able to raise a lot of money.

Sometimes it's good for an organization to eat some humble pie. Truthfully, I wasn't as disciplined as I should have been backstage; too often I was socializing with the guys instead of concentrating on my character. I realized that

I'd lost sight of what helped make the company a success: the fact that I had been so focused as both an actor and an administrator. It was because of this kind of focus and intensity that we'd caught the attention of the legendary Steppenwolf Theatre Company.

Steppenwolf Theatre Company

The members of Steppenwolf Theatre Company are, and probably always will be, the rock stars of Chicago theater. With an ensemble that includes John Malkovich, Gary Sinise, Amy Morton, Frank Galati, Joan Allen, John Mahoney, and Laurie Metcalf, as well as huge production budgets to complement its enormous facilities, Steppenwolf has always been, in my mind, "Hollywood on Halsted Street," and its mythology looms large in the minds of every young actor training or performing in the Midwest. I'm sure most young English thespians hear legendary tales about the early careers of Sir Ben Kingsley, Kenneth Branagh, and Dame Judi Dench. Well, in Chicago, our gospel dealt with the wonder that was Malkovich and Sinise in *True West*, Joan Allen in *Balm in Gilead*, and ensemble member and director Terry Kinney's production of *A Clockwork Orange*.

So you can imagine our shock and excitement when, during Congo Square's very first season, Martha Lavey (Steppenwolf's artistic director) requested a meeting with us to see if we would be interested in working on a collaboration. I'd first met Martha in the lobby of the Chicago Dramatists Theatre when she attended a performance of our inaugural production, *The Piano Lesson*. She'd introduced herself and complimented us on the production, as well as on how we presented ourselves as an organization. What followed, at the end of our first season, was an agreement that our respective ensembles would get together and start reading plays with an eye toward possibly working on a coproduction. As far as we were concerned, we had hit the big time.

However, we quickly came back down to earth as we realized how much work such a collaboration entailed. The strain and frustration of working day jobs, running an education program through the Chicago Park District, and having an ongoing dialogue with Steppenwolf (which had only been going on for a year, but it felt more like 10 years), began to take its toll on both Derrick and me. Finally, Martha agreed to commission our ensemble member Javon Johnson to write a new work to be produced as a collaborative effort by both ensembles. *Breathe* was an original work that dealt with two families—one black, the other white—affected by gun violence and gentrification. Our ensemble read it and thought it was some of Javon's best work; so did Ron OJ Parson, who was to direct the collaboration, and the Steppenwolf ensemble members who were set to appear in the production. However, Martha felt like the play still needed more work and might not go over well with Steppenwolf's audience. Artistic directors at large, financially stable theaters must be acutely aware of their patrons' tastes and aesthetic preferences, setting aside their own enthusiasm for a project if it has the potential to produce disappointing box office numbers or to alienate loyal supporters of the theater. This was a lesson in reality for us, and the two companies went back to the drawing board.

Winter

Preproduction

After setting aside the commissioned piece, our ensemble was exhausted. Derrick and Martha agreed to just produce a published play, since Steppenwolf had already announced that, for the first time in its history, it was mounting a high-profile coproduction with an African American troupe.

I truly believe that Martha had stuck her neck out on our behalf by convincing Steppenwolf to diversify its productions. When the company moved into its new, multimillion-dollar facility on Chicago's Halsted Street in the early nineties, Martha had taken the company to a whole new level by bringing in and nurturing young companies, designers, and directors and giving them access to performance venues such as Steppenwolf's smaller studio and garage spaces.

Yet, out of 30 ensemble members, Steppenwolf had only *one* African American at the time, and you could count on one hand the number of black people in its productions over the years. As the Goodman Theatre produced world premieres by black playwrights such as August Wilson, Regina Taylor, and Wole Soyinka, and Victory Gardens (another Tony Award–winning theater in Chicago) nurtured young black directors and playwrights, Steppenwolf was in danger of being labeled elitist. Martha knew that the company needed diversity. And she knew that in order to move Steppenwolf forward, our companies had to do *something* together.

Personally, I thought we should just "take it on the chin" and push back the collaboration until we could find an appropriate original piece that would highlight both ensembles. If that meant replacing Javon as the playwright, then so be it. I knew it was just too damn difficult to find a published play that catered to our vastly different demographics and actors. But Derrick and the rest of the Congo Square ensemble wanted to commit to the timetable we had originally agreed on—and so, kicking and screaming, I went along with their wishes. The two ensembles decided to do *Wedding Band* by Alice Childress—a play that, to my mind, epitomizes the phrase "museum theater."

Wedding Band by Alice Childress

Synopsis: An interracial love affair turns tragic in World War I–era South Carolina.

Directed by Ron OJ Parson
Set Design by Todd Rosenthal
Lighting Design by Kathy Perkins
Costume Design by Myrna Colley-Lee
Sound and Composition Design by Joe Cerqua
Dramaturge: Nadine Warner
Dialect Coach: Joanna Maclay
Stage Manager: Robert H. Satterlee
Assistant Stage Manager: Alison Ramsey

Featuring: Robert Breuler, Monifa Days, Deanna Dungan, Rae Gray, Ann Joseph, Libya Pugh, TaRon Patton, Jasmine Randle, Will Sims II, Jeannie Moreau, and Rick Snyder.

Postproduction

I think it's safe to say that once the reviews were out, everyone from both ensembles was disappointed—no one more than myself, because the reviews only served to confirm what I'd known in my heart all along: the piece wasn't ideal for the collaboration. As gifted as the actors from both our ensembles were, they still couldn't make a play about miscegenation in South Carolina during WWI relevant to a contemporary Chicago audience. A few Congo Square members had hoped to prove my fears wrong with validation from the critics, but it didn't happen.

To a major theater powerhouse like Steppenwolf, the Mark Taper Forum, or the Public Theater, one bad review is about as significant as a mole on an elephant's ass; organizations like these usually have endowments and loyal subscribers, which means they'll be around for a long time. However, for a young organization like Congo Square, getting a bad or "mixed" review could mean that the game is over. After *A Soldier's Play*, I felt as though we were already in the hole and that the critics had begun to knock the halos off our heads. Before we'd decided to put on *Wedding Band*, Steppenwolf's associate artistic director, Curt Columbus, tried to assure me that this was only the first of many collaborations. I always responded, "If this production isn't a hit, we may not be around long enough for more coproductions." Yet the truth is that it *was* a hit—maybe not artistically, but certainly administratively.

As artists, we want to judge a production first by the impact it has on the public, as we should. Theater, unlike music or the visual arts, needs an audience to exist. However, as a founder of an organization, you sometimes have to measure success by another yardstick. If your company is ever in a position to collaborate with an established Equity theater, please *just do it*! The amount of exposure we received by partnering with a large organization allowed us to apply for larger grants and legitimized us even more in the eyes of funders. Thanks to Steppenwolf's collaboration with us, we were able to receive a $100,000 grant from the Chicago Community Trust, which would later pay for two full-time staff positions.

Despite my disappointment with the production itself, we learned so much about grant writing, fundraising, and marketing from Steppenwolf's administrative staff that I would do it all over again in a heartbeat. One can't put a price on the value of a large Equity house opening its "black book" of local philanthropists. Steppenwolf's director of development,

Sandy Karuschak, and its director of corporate and foundation relations, Sharene Shariatzadeh, were more than gracious and generous in giving their time and expertise. They believed in Congo Square and truly wanted us to be around for the long haul. As did Martha Lavey, without whose renowned vision and passion this collaboration would never have come about at all.

Summer

Preproduction

The third and final piece we chose to do for the season was *Daughters of the Mock* by Judi Ann Mason. It was a play that fit with our "theme" of the season: the art of the ensemble, as epitomized by the work of both Steppenwolf and New York's Negro Ensemble Company. The Negro Ensemble had mounted the national premieres of both *A Soldier's Play* and *Daughters of the Mock*, and we proudly honored that company's legacy. Our production of *Daughters of the Mock* also provided ensemble member Libya Pugh the opportunity to make her directorial debut.

Although our actors had already performed in two productions that season, the only money we'd earned via box office revenue had come from *A Soldier's Tale*; we didn't earn any box office revenue from *Wedding Band* because Steppenwolf had footed the production bill and the play had been performed in its house. We needed to do another production. Unfortunately, we chose a weak script and a bad time to produce it—over the summer. And, as if *that* weren't enough, Derrick and I were both busy doing other projects at the time. He was serving as an assistant director on August Wilson's new play *Gem of the Ocean* at the Mark Taper Forum in Los Angeles, and I was performing in *Race: How Whites and Blacks Think and Feel About the American Obsession* by Studs Terkel. *Race*, which was directed by David Schwimmer, served as the inaugural production of Lookingglass Theatre's new space at the Water Tower Water Works building on Michigan Avenue in downtown Chicago.

The mistake of neglect and abandonment the company had made two years ago with *The Island* was about to happen again, except this time the crime was being committed by the two founding executives.

Daughters of the Mock by Judi Ann Mason

Synopsis: A haunting tale about a grandmother's curse on her womb, meant to protect her female descendants from men.

Directed by Libya Pugh
Set Design by Logan Shunmugam
Lighting Design by JaKyune Seo
Costume Design by Isaac T. King
Sound Design by Matthew Ulm
Stage Manager: Sydney D. Chatman
Assistant Stage Manager: Patience Rayford
History Consultant: Tony Hughes
French Translator: Ozie House-Johnson

Featuring: TaRon Patton, Monifa Days, Tabitha Matthews, China L. Colston, and Chavez Ravine.

Postproduction

This was a play that slipped in through the cracks of our play selection process. We had all become burned out with—and, quite frankly, a little lazy about—choosing the plays we wanted to do coming into year three. Although the second year was an enormous success, it took an awful lot out of our ensemble, and we unfortunately chose to give ourselves a break and just agree to produce this melodrama, even though nobody was all that excited about it. *One thing you can never, ever, do as a theater company is produce a play the company isn't hyped about.* For some strange reason, we thought we could make this production work, but we were wrong. There's definitely truth to that old saying, "If it ain't on the page, it ain't on the stage."

However, that still isn't an excuse to leave an ensemble member who was making her directorial debut hanging. Everything about this show, from the postcard and poster design to the set, lights, and costumes, was a bit second-rate, and Derrick and I were to blame. Usually Derrick was around to crack the whip on the production team, making sure we maximized their talent for the little amount we were paying them. But with him in Los Angeles and me performing seven nights a week across town, the production was abandoned. This is what I mean by becoming too cocky or arrogant when it comes to creating art. With *Daughters of the Mock*, we thought we could easily capture the female audience the way we had with *From the Mississippi Delta*. We also thought we would benefit from the exposure the Steppenwolf collaboration had given us, and we hoped that exposure would translate into box office receipts. But there is no simple formula for creative success.

While *Daughters of the Mock* wasn't a box office flop, it would have sold better had we produced it during the regular theater calendar of September through May. Chicago is a festive city in the summertime, and the last thing most people want to do during its all-too-brief season of good weather is sit inside some theater. That mentality ran through our company as well, and as a result, the production team did not do its best work. The only redeeming factors of the production were the actresses' commitment to the work and the fact that our director grew from the experience. Still, we paid the price of breaking our own rule to use the summer to rest, rejuvenate, and reload for battle.

You're going to make mistakes in the beginning, and your job is to try not to repeat them. That's a lesson Derrick and I both should have learned right away but throughout that entire third season, it was clear that we hadn't. By the end of the run of *Daughters of the Mock*, we had finally learned that when the managing director and the artistic director give only 50 percent of their attention to a production, it's a pretty sure bet that everyone else will follow suit.

TALK-BACK NOTES

- Reviews should only be read *after a show closes*, and they should never cause an ensemble member to become too cocky—or too disheartened.

- Collaborations with large theater ensembles can be beneficial on a multitude of levels, including exposure to a larger audience, another circle of philanthropists, and arts administrators who can help mentor you in your fundraising efforts.

- There is no tried-and-true formula for running a successful theater company. Even if your first couple seasons have been a success, don't allow yourself to think you've figured it all out; stay inspired and hungry.

15

THE LAST VOICE

To earn a living doing what you love to do is a great privilege, and you must never lose sight of that fact. Many people make tons more money than theater artists but they are still unhappy. Even worse, there are those who earn *less* money than us and still go to work every day to perform a job they despise. There will be times when you want to walk away from it all, but remember that you chose to do this work—or, as many people believe, that the work chose you.

By the end of three full seasons, you'll know whether you're fulfilling your destiny or you should move on to something else. For me personally, creating a theater company was my attempt at building a home in which an artist could come and relax among his or her fellows without being judged. An artistic home is important because the only place you're going to grow as an actor is in an environment where you're free to experiment and fall flat on your face away from the piercing eyes of a critic or a paying audience. The mission statement and culture of your company should prepare patrons for what your company's willing to attempt. Sometimes, by casting against type, an artistic director challenges the ensemble, which in turn challenges the audience. What audiences and critics should see is the end result of a sometimes grueling creative process—a process that when done with absolute commitment and concentration, lends itself to art.

I advise you to be bold in the productions you choose to execute. Theater can speak to modern audiences and communities in ways that cinema cannot. Do plays about race, politics, religion, homosexuality, time travel, AIDS, and so forth—subjects that Hollywood rarely explores (well, perhaps time travel is the exception). You and your comrades have a huge responsibility to yourselves and to your audience to do cutting-edge work that will provoke, inspire, challenge, and, of course, entertain. An underlying current running through your company should be the desire to develop the next Lloyd Richards, Arthur Miller, Julie Taymor, David Mamet, or August Wilson. Twenty years from now, you'll be able to look back on your body of work and realize what an adventure you've had.

From the Playwright

On Sunday, October 2, 2005, American theater grew silent as she lost yet another son, when August Wilson passed. Having lost Arthur Miller a few months earlier, the entire nation took notice as its greatest living playwrights made their final bows and closed the curtain on an era. In Mr. Wilson, Congo Square lost its biggest fan, mentor, benefactor, and—most important—friend.

The theater is the last true voice of the people. Unlike films and television shows, which have to go through so many hands before you come up with a final story, a play usually stays true to what the playwright originally intended. The director, actors, and designers all team up to help illuminate the play's theme and offer it to the audience. What the community receives from a great theater company doing exceptional work is art at its most potent.

The screenwriter isn't as fortunate as the playwright. There are three version of a screenplay: the one that's written, the one that's shot, and the one that's edited. A film that audiences view at a movie theater could be light years away from the movie the writer initially anticipated. There are simply too many "hands" involved in making a movie. That is why theater represents the last voice of the people—because in it resides a built-in *control* factor.

The first playwright was actually an actor named Thespis who happened to break from the Greek chorus and create his own dialogue. Many great playwrights start off as actors, only to evolve into writers. Shakespeare, Molière, Brecht, and Mamet took it a step further by working with their own theater companies. All of these extraordinary and gifted scribes penned some of their best material for actors they already knew.

During the start of his professional career, while working under Lloyd Richards at Yale, even August Wilson wrote material for such powerful actors as Charles S. Dutton, James Earl Jones, and Charlie Brown. It was because of his respect for Charles "Roc" Dutton that Mr. Wilson created one of his most memorable characters, Boy Willie in *The Piano Lesson*.

Today Mamet still continues to work with actor William H. Macy at their Atlantic Theatre Company in New York. Together, the two have developed an entire new "style" of acting that they teach to hundreds of students. Another emerging playwright doing great work with an ensemble is Stephen Adly Guirgis. His *Jesus Hopped the "A" Train* and *Our Lady of 121th Street* are wonderful pieces written for the actors at Labyrinth Theatre Company.

It's very difficult to write a play, so when someone accomplishes such a task, your job is to help that person bring the work to life. Find out why he or she wrote the piece and who its target audience is. If, at some point, someone in your ensemble wants to try his or her hand at writing a piece—be it an original play or an adaptation of a great novel—the ensemble must encourage and support that person. Keep in mind that many great works of the theater came about as a result of the relationship between a playwright and a specific group of actors for whom he or she wrote.

From the Director

The director's job is to compose the actors and designers in a synchronized rhythm that plays to the tune of what is written on the page. A good director (like any real artist) sees what's in between the lines and stage directions of the play to give it a real heartbeat. The director's job is to inspire, enlighten, challenge, and even sometimes protect his or her fellow artists and collaborators. In addition, it's often difficult for an actor to see if the choices he or she is making are coming across effectively to the audience, so directors also act as the "third eye" of the actor, to make sure that what the audience receives from a performance is clear. More than anyone else in the ensemble, a director is responsible for conveying the theme of the play to the audience. The best stage directors are historians, critics, coaches, and managers.

Communication is key if one wants to consider a serious career as a director of the stage. The manner in which you speak to actors could be crucial to determining what kind of performance you bring out of them. Once the director casts a production and hires the actor who's best qualified for the role, the fault lies with the director if that actor doesn't deliver. On a film, a director must supervise so many technical details and such an enormous cast and crew that he or she rarely has time to spend working with an actor who needs attention. But in theater, the director has no such obligations to use as an excuse; working with actors should be high on his or her priority list.

I should point out that the stage does have it share of visionaries—Mary Zimmerman, Julie Taymor, Peter Brook, and others—whose stage compositions are what make their productions stunning. Some of these compositions feel cinematic on stage, and the acting can sometimes become a secondary component of the production. These conceptual directors, who are known for changing the casting of a play or its setting, oftentimes run into problems with playwrights who believe that the director isn't being true to their intentions. Probably the most famous such bout between a director and a playwright occurred in the American Repertory Theater's production of *Endgame* by Samuel Beckett, which was directed by Joanne Akalaitis. The production included two black actors in the lead roles, and Akalaitis tweaked the setting of the environment. This raised numerous debates as to how much creative license a stage director has on a living playwright's work. It's a debate that will most certainly continue well into the 21st century.

Unlike their film counterparts, who screen movies for audiences only after the actors have finished shooting, the footage has been edited together, and there's little time or money left for reshoots, theater directors incorporate audience response into their process during previews, when it can still play a huge part in determining the production's final form.

There's an old saying among filmmakers that movies are never finished, only abandoned. Well, in the theater, directors never abandon their productions—they finish them.

From the Actors

Theatrical actors are the best actors around because they are the toughest. They endure everything film actors experience and more—all without the safety nets of personal assistants, publicists, makeup artists, microphones, great editors, or cinematographers. Most do it for the love of the game instead of a desire for fame or fortune, so they have a tendency to have more respect for the process. However, once in a while you will come across people who love *themselves* in the art more than the art in themselves. People should get involved in the arts only if they truly have something to say or offer the community. We all are in service to the work, and we must never lose sight of that. The theater is one of the last places where an audience is willing to accept, or at least hear, a "message" in the form of entertainment. Our ability to offer that message is an enormous privilege that shouldn't be taken lightly.

If you find yourself working with an actor who is not collaborating well with his or her peers (and we've all been there), it's best to just focus on your own role and dig in a little deeper. Hopefully, your discipline will inspire the actor to get back on track.

As a theatrical actor, you share the same time and space as your audience, and it all plays out right in front of your eyes. Nothing captures the imagination more than a live event, and actors are the vehicles that deliver that experience to the people. The best work is done when actors in a repertory or ensemble grow together and learn one another's rhythms.

As your ensemble matures, it's comforting to remember that despite the highs and lows, you are trekking on the same journey taken by the Moscow Art Theatre and the Royal Shakespeare Company.

Keep in mind that you have chosen a great, noble profession that is steeped in history and tradition. As your company continues to grow and produce, you are leaving footprints in the sand and writing your own history as it relates to the community. You have the training, the discipline, and the desire, so don't let anything stop you from living your dream of becoming a professional actor. The world needs more genuine theater companies that are not obsessed with growth and expansion but are instead more interested in society and in helping us all figure out what it means to be human. In order for that to happen, a theater needs actors who are confident, generous, and dedicated—not only to themselves but to the organization, as well.

To the People

After scanning the cultural landscape of Chicago, our hunch paid off. Congo Square offered the people something they weren't getting from other theater companies. In only three roller coaster years, we were well on our way to becoming a pillar in the community. By season four, our operating budget was a staggering $200,000, and we were able to hire a full-time executive director and finally place the artistic director on salary. I also moved us from Union Park to the Athenaeum Theatre, a larger, much more comfortable office space on the North Side that has hosted other arts organizations, including at the time Lookingglass Theatre Company. That's your job as the founder of a company: to figure out what it is, exactly, that you're going to offer the public and to deliver it, come hell or high water. The more you involve the company in the community at large, the more your company becomes branded into the community's collective psyche.

Be sure to attend other arts events, such as dance concerts, gallery openings, concerts, and even live sporting events. The work of these professional artists and athletes will keep you refueled and inspired. Visiting a great museum or attending a great concert can be like drinking a tall glass of water as you run the marathon of a professional career in live theater.

Whether you're in a big city or a small town, you'll always find people who want good theater. Your training makes you more than qualified to bring great professional theater to the people. Don't wait for someone to give you permission to act; get up and do it! When you do, your agenda and those of your comrades should be one and the same—to leave the community a better place than it was before you arrived.

APPENDIX

Important Organizations
for Assistance

Actors' Equity Offices

Actors' Equity Association (National Headquarters/ Eastern Region)
165 West 46th Street
New York, NY 10036
(212) 869-8530
Fax: (212) 719-9815
www.actorsequity.org

Actors' Equity Association (Central Region)
125 South Clark Street, Suite 1500
Chicago, IL 60603
(312) 641-0393
Fax: (312) 641-6365
www.actorsequity.org/aboutequity/central.asp

Actor's Equity Association (Eastern Region satellite office)
10319 Orangewood Boulevard
Orlando, FL 32821
(407) 345-8600

Fax: (407) 345-1522
www.actorsequity.org/aboutequity/eastern.asp

Actors' Equity Association (Western Region)
6755 Hollywood Blvd., 5th Floor
Los Angeles, CA 90028
(323) 978-8080
Fax: (323) 978-8081
www.actorsequity.org/aboutequity/western.asp

Attorneys

Volunteer Lawyers for the Arts
Primarily represents artists in the New York area
1 East 53rd Street, 6th Floor
New York, NY 10022
(212) 319-2787
Fax: (212) 752-6575
www.vlany.org

Lawyers for the Creative Arts
Primarily represents artists in the Midwest
213 Institute Place, Suite 403
Chicago, IL 60610
(312) 649-4111
Fax: (312) 944-2195
www.law-arts.org

California Lawyers for the Arts (Northern Region)
*Primarily represents artists in San Francisco and
other Northern California areas*
Fort Mason Center, C-255
San Francisco, CA 94123

(415) 775-7200
Fax: (415) 775-1143
www.calawyersforthearts.org

California Lawyers for the Arts (Southern Region)
*Primarily represents artists in Los Angeles and other
Southern California areas*
1641 18th Street
Santa Monica, CA 90404
(310) 998-5590
Fax: (310) 998-5594
www.calawyersforthearts.org

Washington Area Lawyers for the Arts
Primarily represents artists in the Washington, D.C., area
901 New York Avenue NW, Suite P1
Washington, DC 20001-4413
(202)-289-4440
www.thewala.org

INDEX